PERFECT PARTIES

PERFECT PARTIES

Entertaining with Southern Style

FROM THE EDITORS OF SOUTHERN LADY

Copyright ©2024 by Hoffman Media

All rights reserved. No part of this book may be reproduced or transmitted in any form or by any means, electronic or mechanical, including photocopying, or by any information storage and retrieval system, without permission in writing from Hoffman Media. Reviewers may quote brief passages for specific inclusion in a magazine or newspaper.

Hoffman Media
2323 2nd Avenue North
Birmingham, AL 35203
hoffmanmedia.com

ISBN 979-8-9899185-4-6
Printed in China

83 press

Contents

8 | FOREWORD

10
CHAPTER 1:
HOSTESS ESSENTIALS

20
CHAPTER 2:
FAMILY & FELLOWSHIP

- 22 Friendship Blooms
- 30 Refined Celebration
- 38 Open-Air Idyll
- 48 Mother's Day Memories
- 56 Together Again
- 66 Flowers & Finery
- 78 Lunch in the Garden

88
CHAPTER 3:
LOVE IS IN THE AIR

- 90 Enchanted Evening
- 98 Sweet as Honey
- 106 Something Blue
- 116 Soirée for Sweethearts
- 124 Love Blossoms
- 132 Blissful Beginnings
- 142 Happily Ever After

152
CHAPTER 4:
CELEBRATIONS OF CHILDHOOD

- 154 Bundle of Joy
- 164 Daintiest Delights
- 170 Oh Happy Day
- 180 Baskets & Bounty
- 192 Sunny Sixteen
- 200 Itty Bitty Pretty One
- 208 Dreamy Dessert Social

218 | RECIPE INDEX
219 | CREDITS & ACKNOWLEDGMENTS

Foreword

BY LYDIA MENZIES OF LYDIA MENZIES CELEBRATES

Have you ever attended the perfect party? You know the one—where the hostess was gracious, the partygoers were festive and chatty, the food was fabulous, and it was over all too soon? *Perfect Parties* will help you apply all of those attributes to each of your soirées to create a fabulous fête every time.

Can you have more than one perfect party? Of course you can! That's the goal: consistently delivering a welcoming experience, knowing what to serve and how to serve it beautifully, for the biggest milestones of life or the simplest moments among family and friends.

Is there an exact science to a perfect party? Never. That's what makes each one uniquely special. But there is a framework you can follow to help you host flawless events for the milestone moments that reflect traditions. That structure is outlined in this book, serving not only as a lovely reference for now but also as a guide that can be passed on for generations to come.

For instance, as you celebrate the little ones, they will learn the basics of hospitality that will grow into a deeper appreciation for the value of celebrating others. It becomes second nature, and the traditions continue to carry on among future friends and families. As you celebrate the gifts of friendship, marriage, motherhood, birthdays, anniversaries, and other significant moments, *Perfect Parties* is here to guide you like a dear grandmother looking over your shoulder with a gentle nudge and an enthusiastic "Well done!" all rolled into one.

Perfection is based on perception, and if your guests feel loved and embraced, you have succeeded in hosting the perfect party. And remember, no one but you will ever know if the flowers wilted a bit or the decorated cookies were lost in the mail and had to be replaced with something simpler. Those are the perfectly imperfect parts that ultimately lead to a confident hostess who realizes the true importance is the experience created, the fellowship shared, the memories made, and the occasions remembered. That, my friend, is party perfection.

So, dive in and soak up the knowledge you'll glean from the pages of this beautiful book. Let yourself be influenced by the thoughtfulness of the celebrations and inspired by the visual artistry. Trust yourself to plan your own version of a perfect party with these tried-and-true recipes and creative table settings sprung from the pages of *Southern Lady* magazine over the years.

You will be ready to open your home and your heart to create experiences that we all know will be the best version of your own perfect parties!

1

Hostess Essentials

WITH OUR REPERTOIRE OF ENTERTAINING MUST-HAVES, PLAN MEMORABLE EVENTS FOR ANY NUMBER OF GUESTS WITH PEACE OF MIND.

How to Stock Your Party Pantry

Fill your cupboard with an array of versatile china, linens, and other tableware that will keep party preparation smooth and seamless.

Entertaining at home is easier when you don't have to start from scratch. With a well-stocked party pantry, you'll spend less time preparing for guests and more time enjoying their company. Be ready to welcome them when opportunity knocks by keeping these fundamentals at your fingertips.

A RANGE OF PLATTERS

Serving pieces are heavy-hitting multitaskers for any hostess. Amassing a variety of platters and bowls in multiple sizes ensures you'll have a dish to hold whatever type of food you choose. White porcelain, creamware, or ironstone can easily be dressed up or down and will go with everything while providing an appealing presentation for foods of all kinds. Or unify disparate pieces by limiting them to a monochromatic palette that suits your décor. You can also embrace the collected look, mixing and matching vintage pieces and modern finds as the occasion dictates.

A VARIETY OF GLASSES

Having a collection of vessels in which to distribute beverages is essential. Basics to consider include rocks glasses, highball or Collins glasses, wineglasses, and Champagne flutes, but some can serve dual purposes, like water glasses that work equally well for sweet tea. Expand your array over time by adding glassware made for specific drinks you enjoy serving, and remember to keep ample coffee cups and teacups at the ready.

VASES OF EVERY SHAPE AND SIZE

Fresh flowers are a surefire way to add color and elegance to a space. It's not uncommon for visitors to gift these to a hostess upon arrival, so make sure you have a few different vases handy that will suit the scale of any bouquet. No need to break out the crystal for a casual occasion—pitchers, jars, or even glass bottles work well for displaying blooms at a moment's notice.

PLENTY OF LINENS

A basic linen wardrobe includes two to three tablecloths, dinner and beverage napkins, place mats, and a runner. Crisply ironed linens in neutral hues that mesh with your dishware are a timeless way to bring sophistication to any gathering. Add some extras in festive colors so your party pantry will be ready for any season or holiday. To dress up linens even further, have them embellished with a monogram or a custom embroidery motif. Good-quality paper beverage napkins with a pretty design are useful to have on hand for very casual get-togethers.

FLATWARE AND SERVING UTENSILS

Depending on how large a crowd you typically host, you'll want to have enough silver or stainless steel salad forks, dinner forks, knives, and spoons to go around. Consider buying mismatched silver at vintage markets and antiques shops, which is affordable and lends extra visual interest. Other essentials include serving spoons (both solid and pierced), serving forks, salad servers, sugar spoons, spreaders, small ladles, cake servers, and butter knives. If you often give very dressy dinner parties or luncheons, it can be fun to collect old-fashioned items such as demitasse spoons, olive forks, tomato and asparagus servers, and iced beverage spoons.

Setting a Gracious Table

Nothing says "Welcome!" like a beautifully set table or an artfully arranged buffet. Color schemes, centerpieces, and decorative fancies are boundless, but these basic guidelines will ensure your tableau feels on point for the occasion at hand.

FOR A FORMAL MEAL

Although setting a formal table once meant a vast spread of specialty pieces such as fish forks and sherry glasses, today's elegant affairs are a good deal more streamlined. Begin by centering a charger or service plate at each place setting, topped with the dinner and then the salad plate. If you are using a soup bowl, it goes atop the salad plate. While the napkin traditionally is placed to the left or on top of the plates, creative folds and table décor give you additional options, such as tucking it inside a water goblet.

Arrange forks to the left of the plate in the order of use, with the salad fork on the outside and dinner fork closer in. The knife and then the spoon go to the right of the plate, and the blade of each knife should face inward. Dessert spoons or forks can be placed above the plate or simply brought out with dessert.

Position each water goblet directly above the tip of the knife; a wineglass or tea glass sits to the right. Bread-and-butter plates should be placed above the tines of the forks, with the butter knife resting horizontally across the center.

FOR A CASUAL MEAL

The approach to an informal table is a bit more relaxed, with leeway for creative placement of pieces such as napkins and glassware. Place a folded napkin to the left of each dinner plate (atop the place mat, if you're using one) and lay the forks directly on it. If you opt for a napkin ring instead, you can set the napkin on the plate, to the left of the setting, or angled above the forks. As with formal settings, the salad fork is farthest left, and the knife and spoon should be placed to the right of the plate. Put a water glass directly above or slightly offset to the knife.

FOR A BUFFET

First, decide if a single-sided or double-sided buffet is appropriate for the size and style of your gathering. For larger crowds, the latter approach keeps service moving smoothly by allowing guests to form two lines, one on each side.

In both cases, place a stack of dinner plates or salad plates at one end to mark the starting point. Beside them, arrange cold or room-temperature foods such as cheese and fruit platters, salads, and crudité. Next come hot sides and main dishes, plus any sauces and condiments that accompany them. Place rolls or sliced breads and butter toward the end; finish with utensils and napkins. Some hosts like to bundle flatware in the napkins for ease.

It's preferable to serve desserts from a separate station, complete with dessert plates or bowls and forks or spoons. Beverages should be served from a dedicated spot such as a side table or home bar.

Tips for an Inviting Atmosphere

A few finishing touches are all it takes to set a pleasant tone that puts guests at ease upon arrival.

KEEP LIGHTING SOFT. Dim overhead fixtures and switch on lamps and sconces for a gentle glow. When it comes to candles, select votives and tapers in neutral tones or colors that blend well with your décor. Avoid those with strong scents, especially near food. If smoke or fire safety are concerns, use flameless LED varieties. Depending on the occasion, string lights or paper lanterns can add to the ambience as well.

FINE-TUNE THE TEMPERATURE. For a houseful of guests, set the thermostat two or three degrees below your usual temperature. You can always adjust it later if necessary. On a sweltering day, keep shades and curtains drawn before the party starts to offset the extra warmth.

SET THE MOOD WITH MUSIC. Make a playlist in harmony with your event—instrumental jazz for a cocktail gathering; upbeat pop for a cookout; mellow classical for a tea party. Or if you're honoring a special guest, play a medley of his or her favorite songs. Adjust the volume so guests can hear the music clearly but not so loud that conversation becomes difficult.

PLAY UP THE SEASON. Flourishes appropriate to the time of year underscore the festive air. If it's chilly out, light the fireplace or an outdoor firepit before guests arrive. In warmer months, scatter bud vases filled with blossoms from your garden or the farmers' market. A display of brilliant leaves and gourds brings the magic of autumn indoors.

Hospitality in a Hurry

With a hint of foresight and a dash of composure, you'll be ready to host an impromptu get-together in gracious style.

When friends call on you at a moment's notice, the surprise may spur a frenzy of tidying up and rummaging for refreshments. Resist the urge to drag out cleaning supplies or apologize for seeming unprepared, and instead, relish the unexpected rendezvous by putting your best foot forward in a pinch. Adding a few simple tasks to your daily life and keeping delights on hand will ensure you are cool, calm, and collected when opening the door to drop-in guests.

STOCK THE KITCHEN WITH EASY-TO-SERVE GOODIES.

Purchase nonperishable nibbles and various beverages now and then on routine grocery store trips. Nuts, crackers, and cheese straws are good pantry essentials, while shelf-stable dips and pickled tidbits can be kept chilled in the refrigerator. Pick up an assortment of teas, flavored sparkling water, and a bottle each of red and white wine so you'll have a range of choices to offer on the spot.

KEEP YOUR LINEN COLLECTION WASHED AND PRESSED.

While paper cocktail napkins have their place, crisp linens make any occasion feel special, however impromptu. A pretty cloth or embroidered textile lends élan in a snap and also disguises a less-than-pristine tabletop. Launder and iron or steam all linens before neatly storing them so a variety of options are always at hand.

REGULARLY FRESHEN GUEST BATHROOMS AND OUTDOOR LIVING AREAS.

Check to ensure the powder room remains stocked with toilet tissue and hand soap. Little luxuries, like a fragrance diffuser and fluffy hand towels, set an inviting tone. On the patio or porch, take a few extra minutes during your typical housekeeping routine to dust off furnishings, wipe down surfaces, and tend potted herbs or plants. These small efforts go a long way to keeping both spaces prepped and inviting.

TURN ON LIGHTS, BURN CANDLES, AND PLAY MUSIC FOR INSTANT AMBIENCE.

If it's evening or if the day is gray, switch on lamps and light candles with subtle fragrances. The luminous glow and pleasant aroma combine for a cozy feel, setting you and your company at ease. Soothing background music can elevate the mood as well.

RELAX AND APPRECIATE THE OPPORTUNITY TO RECONNECT.

Like any other entertaining scenario, the most important part of greeting guests is making them feel genuinely welcome. Put aside any trepidation and focus on the joys that are sure to ensue from this unanticipated visit. No matter if they sit a spell over coffee or linger until the wee hours, more than anything else, you will both remember and cherish the time spent together.

Party Planning Checklist

With so many decisions to make and tasks to handle, planning a gathering can feel daunting for even the most enthusiastic of hosts. Use our checklist to streamline preparations and keep track of what to do when—and remember to build in time to relax on the day of the event so you are at your best when guests arrive.

Two Months in Advance
- [ ] Decide on a theme and set a budget.
- [ ] Book a caterer if you plan to use one.
- [ ] Arrange for outside help such as housecleaning if necessary.

One Month to Three Weeks in Advance
- [ ] Finalize the date and time if you have not done so.
- [ ] Draw up your guest list. A good rule of thumb is that 75 to 80 percent of invitees will attend.
- [ ] Order or create and send invitations.
- [ ] Plan your menu and décor.
- [ ] Order custom items such as a cake, a balloon arch, flower arrangements, or printed accents.

Two Weeks in Advance
- [ ] Make a grocery list.
- [ ] Inventory cookware, serveware, and floral containers; order or shop for any extras.
- [ ] Purchase decorations.

One Week in Advance
- [ ] Inventory linens and launder or dry clean as needed.
- [ ] Shop for foods that will keep until the party. These include frozen and shelf-stable items as well as beverages.
- [ ] Clean your house (or have it cleaned).
- [ ] Create a music playlist.
- [ ] Follow up on any missing RSVPs.

One to Two Days in Advance
- [ ] Clean out the refrigerator to make space for party fare.
- [ ] Shop for last-minute grocery items.
- [ ] Clean and polish china, glassware, and silver.
- [ ] Designate a space for coats and bags.
- [ ] Rearrange furniture and seating as needed.
- [ ] Confirm delivery times with caterers or other vendors.
- [ ] Prepare any foods that can be made ahead.
- [ ] Buy the flowers you plan to arrange yourself. Be sure to clip all stems at a 45-degree angle when placing in water to keep the blooms looking their very best.
- [ ] Put out decorations and write place cards.
- [ ] Set the table or arrange tableware on a buffet. To guard against dust, you can lay tall glassware and other breakables carefully on their sides and then drape a clean sheet over the table and remove it closer to the time of the event.

Day of the Party
- [ ] Tidy up and spot clean your house.
- [ ] Empty the dishwasher and trash bins.
- [ ] Buy ice if needed and chill beverages.
- [ ] Finish any last food preparation.
- [ ] Turn on music, adjust lighting, and light candles.
- [ ] Set out food just before guests arrive.

2
Family & Fellowship

MERRIMENT ABOUNDS AT THESE GATHERINGS THAT TEEM WITH SCRUMPTIOUS SPREADS AND THE DELIGHT OF GOOD COMPANY.

Friendship Blooms

CONGREGATE IN THE GARDEN TO MAKE USE OF THE BEST AND BRIGHTEST BLOSSOMS AT A FLORAL-ARRANGING FÊTE.

ARTFULLY ARRANGED

Amid the flourishing beauty of an airy backyard, conversation flows freely as guests follow a demonstration in crafting a beautiful bouquet, jotting down notes in handmade booklets. A color scheme of soft pink and lavender matches the delicate tints of perennial favorites like peonies, hydrangeas, and roses, while satin ribbons and handwritten place cards enhance the setting's aura. After an alfresco meal, the group moves to the petite worktable, where attendees can select from an assortment of fresh cuttings to assemble their own blossoming masterpieces.

Elderflower Rosé Wine Spritzer
MAKES 10 TO 12 SERVINGS

2 (750ml) bottles rosé sparkling wine
2 cups elderflower liqueur
1 cup vodka
1 cup fresh lemon juice
Botanical ice cubes (see Kitchen Tip)
5 cups lemon sparkling water
Garnish: sliced lemon, edible flowers

1. In a large pitcher, stir together rosé, elderflower liqueur, vodka, and lemon juice.
2. Fill serving glasses with ice. Pour about 1 cup rosé mixture into each glass. Top each with about ½ cup sparkling water. Garnish with lemon and flowers, if desired.

KITCHEN TIP:
To make botanical ice cubes, place edible flower petals or mint and lemon zest in the wells of ice cube trays. Fill wells with water and freeze at least 24 hours.

Mini Crab Quiches
MAKES 10 TO 12 SERVINGS

2 (14.1-ounce) packages refrigerated piecrusts
½ cup heavy whipping cream
2 large eggs
⅛ teaspoon kosher salt
½ cup fresh jumbo lump crabmeat, picked free of shell
½ cup shredded Gruyère cheese
2 tablespoons sliced fresh chives
1 teaspoon chopped fresh thyme
Garnish: lump crabmeat, fresh thyme sprigs

1. Preheat oven to 450°.
2. On a lightly floured surface, unroll piecrust dough. Using a 4-inch round cutter, cut 6 rounds from each piecrust. Transfer each round into a 2¼-inch fluted tartlet pan, pressing into bottom and up sides. Using the handle of a wooden spoon, gently press dough into indentations in sides of pans. Trim excess dough. Using a fork, prick the bottom of each tartlet. Place tartlet pans on a rimmed baking sheet. Refrigerate for 15 minutes.
3. Place a small piece of parchment paper in center of each prepared tartlet pan, letting ends extend over edges of pan, and fill with ceramic pie weights. Bake for 10 minutes. Carefully remove pie weights and parchment paper. Reduce oven temperature to 350°.
4. In a medium bowl, whisk together cream, egg, and salt.
5. In a small bowl, stir together crab, cheese, chives, and thyme. Divide crab mixture among tartlet shells. Carefully pour egg mixture over crab mixture.
6. Bake until filling is set and slightly puffed, 12 to 15 minutes. Let cool slightly on a wire rack before carefully removing quiches from pans. Garnish with crab and thyme, if desired.

Perfect Parties | 27

Spring Garden Seven-Layer Salad
MAKES 10 TO 12 SERVINGS

1 (10-ounce) can garbanzo beans, drained and rinsed
1½ cups cooked quinoa
2 tablespoons chopped fresh parsley
1 tablespoon chopped fresh mint
1 tablespoon chopped fresh dill
1 (5-ounce) bag fresh spring mix
2 cups sliced fresh endive
2 cups sliced radishes
⅓ cup thinly sliced red onion
1 (4-ounce) container crumbled feta cheese
1 (5.3-ounce) container 2% plain Greek yogurt
1 teaspoon lemon zest
¼ cup fresh lemon juice
1 tablespoon tahini
1 teaspoon kosher salt
½ teaspoon ground black pepper
Garnish: fresh dill sprigs

1. In a medium bowl, stir together beans, quinoa, parsley, mint, and dill. Spread in an even layer in a glass trifle dish.
2. Layer spring mix, endive, radish, red onion, and cheese on top of quinoa mixture.
3. In a small bowl, whisk together yogurt, lemon zest and juice, tahini, salt, and pepper. Drizzle over salad. Garnish with dill, if desired.

Apricot Crumble Bars
MAKES 10 TO 12 SERVINGS

3 cups quick-cooking oats
1 cup all-purpose flour
1 cup lightly packed light brown sugar
½ teaspoon baking soda
¼ teaspoon kosher salt
⅛ teaspoon ground cinnamon
¾ cup unsalted butter, melted
2 (15-ounce) cans apricots in light syrup, drained and diced
2 (8.2-ounce) jars apricot fruit spread*
2 teaspoons lemon zest

1. Preheat oven to 350°. Line a 13x9-inch baking pan with aluminum foil, extending ends of foil over edges of pan about 2 inches. Spray pan with cooking spray. Set aside.
2. In a large bowl, stir together oats, flour, brown sugar, baking soda, salt, and cinnamon. Add melted butter, tossing to combine. Reserve 1 cup oats mixture. Press remaining oats mixture into bottom of prepared pan.
3. Bake until set, 12 to 15 minutes.
4. In a small bowl, stir together apricots, fruit spread, and lemon zest. Gently spread apricot mixture over crust. Sprinkle with reserved oats mixture.
5. Bake until lightly browned and bubbly, 35 to 40 minutes. Let cool completely on a wire rack. Using foil ends, remove from pan. Trim edges, if desired. Cut into squares. Refrigerate until ready to serve.

*We used Bonne Maman Intense Apricot Fruit Spread.

Perfect Parties | 29

Refined Celebration

CHEERFULNESS THRIVES AT THIS FANCIFUL BIRTHDAY LUNCHEON PLANNED WITH AN EYE FOR SOPHISTICATION.

LAUGHTER AND LIGHT

Convivial chatter echoes among companions in this space cloaked in a dreamy palette. Blue-and-white dishware lends classic elegance alongside floral arrangements tinted with feminine shades of fuchsia and blush. Candlesticks modeled after feathered friends present an exotic touch with towering aqua tapers, while geometric motifs in the tablecloth and rattan place mats accent the stylish tableau. Partygoers dine on a light menu of soup and salad followed by delicate pink cupcakes as the guest of honor opens pretty parcels, delighting in the thoughtful gifts bestowed.

Perfect Parties | 33

Cherry-Lemon Sparkler
MAKES 6 TO 8 SERVINGS

1½ cups sugar
1½ cups water
2 cups fresh lemon juice
4 cups sparkling water
3 tablespoons grenadine
Garnish: maraschino cherries, lemon slices

1. In a small saucepan, bring sugar and 1½ cups water to a boil over medium-high heat. Reduce heat and simmer until sugar dissolves. Let cool to room temperature.
2. In a large pitcher, whisk together cooled simple syrup and lemon juice. Fill each serving glass with ice. Divide lemon juice mixture between glasses. Top each evenly with sparkling water. Top each with grenadine. Garnish with cherries and lemon, if desired.

> **KITCHEN TIP:**
> Make this cocktail by adding 1½ ounces gin to each serving.

Watercress Salad with Lemon and Almonds
MAKES 6 TO 8 SERVINGS

2 (4-ounce) bags fresh watercress
¼ cup thinly sliced red onion
2 tablespoons Champagne vinegar
1 tablespoon olive oil
¼ teaspoon lightly packed lemon zest
1 teaspoon fresh lemon juice
1 teaspoon Dijon mustard
1 teaspoon honey
¼ teaspoon kosher salt
¼ teaspoon ground black pepper
¼ cup chopped roasted and salted Marcona almonds

1. In a large bowl, combine watercress and onion.
2. In a small bowl, whisk together vinegar, olive oil, lemon zest and juice, mustard, honey, salt, and pepper. Drizzle over watercress mixture and gently toss to combine. Sprinkle with almonds.

Roasted Red Pepper Soup with Shrimp
MAKES 6 SERVINGS

2 tablespoons unsalted butter
2 cups chopped yellow onion
3 cloves garlic, chopped
1 cup chopped carrot
½ cup chopped celery
7 cups chicken broth
4 (12-ounce) jars roasted red peppers, drained
1 tablespoon kosher salt, divided
4 cups cubed French bread
2 tablespoons olive oil, divided
1 cup shredded smoked Gouda cheese
18 large fresh shrimp, peeled and deveined
Crème fraîche, for topping
Garnish: ground black pepper, sliced fresh chives, fresh chive blossoms*

1. In a Dutch oven, melt butter over medium heat. Add onion and garlic; cook, stirring occasionally, until softened and fragrant, 5 minutes. Add carrot and celery; cook until softened, 5 to 7 minutes. Add broth, roasted peppers, and 2 teaspoons salt; bring to a boil. Reduce heat and simmer until vegetables are very tender, 15 to 20 minutes. Using an immersion blender, blend soup until smooth.
2. Preheat oven to 400°. Line a rimmed baking sheet with parchment paper.
3. Arrange bread cubes on prepared baking sheet in an even layer. Drizzle with 1 tablespoon olive oil and sprinkle with ½ teaspoon salt.
4. Bake until golden brown and toasted, 10 minutes. Sprinkle with cheese. Continue baking until cheese is melted, about 2 minutes more.
5. In a medium skillet, heat remaining 1 tablespoon olive oil over medium-high heat. Season shrimp with remaining ½ teaspoon salt. Add shrimp to pan and cook, turning occasionally, until pink and firm, 5 to 7 minutes.

6. Top servings of soup with crème fraîche, Gouda croutons, and shrimp. Garnish with black pepper and chives, if desired.

*We used Gourmet Sweet Botanicals chive blossoms.

Angel Food Cupcakes with Swiss Meringue Buttercream
MAKES 12

½ cup bleached cake flour
⅔ cup sugar, divided
5 large egg whites
½ teaspoon cream of tartar
¼ teaspoon kosher salt
½ teaspoon vanilla extract
Swiss Meringue Buttercream (recipe follows)
Garnish: pink edible glitter

1. Preheat oven to 350°. Line a 12-cup muffin pan with paper liners.
2. In a medium bowl, sift together flour and ⅓ cup sugar.
3. In the bowl of a stand mixer fitted with the whisk attachment, beat egg whites at medium-high speed until foamy, about 1 minute. Slowly add remaining ⅓ cup sugar. Increase mixer speed to high; immediately add cream of tartar and salt. Add vanilla, and beat until soft peaks form, about 2 minutes.
4. Transfer egg white mixture to a large bowl. Using a large balloon whisk, fold in flour mixture in 4 additions just until combined. Divide batter among muffin liners. Run a butter knife through batter to release any air bubbles, and smooth tops.
5. Bake until firm to the touch, lightly browned, and an instant-read thermometer inserted into the center registers 200°, 10 to 12 minutes. Let cool completely.
6. Transfer Swiss Meringue Buttercream to a piping bag, fitted with an open-star piping tip (Wilton 1M). Pipe buttercream evenly onto cupcakes. Garnish with edible glitter, if desired.

SWISS MERINGUE BUTTERCREAM
MAKES ABOUT 3 CUPS

½ cup egg whites (about 4 large eggs)
¾ cup sugar
1 cup unsalted butter, softened
½ teaspoon vanilla extract
Pink gel food coloring* (optional)

1. In the bowl of a stand mixer fitted with the whisk attachment, beat egg whites and sugar until frothy.
2. Place bowl over a small saucepan of simmering water. Whisk mixture constantly until sugar dissolves and a candy thermometer registers 160°, about 2 minutes. Return bowl to mixer and beat at high speed until stiff peaks form. Add butter, 1 tablespoon at a time, beating well after each addition. Add vanilla and food coloring (if using) until desired color is reached. (We used 4 dots of food coloring using a toothpick.)

*We used Sunny Side Up Bakery Soft Pink squeeze gel food coloring.

KITCHEN TIP:
If the butter starts to seize up or the icing gets too cold, place the mixing bowl over a saucepan of simmering water and whisk constantly until smooth.

Perfect Parties

Open-Air Idyll

A LIGHTHEARTED MEAL IN A CLEARING DAPPLED WITH SHADE
EMBODIES THE EASYGOING ÉLAN OF WARM AFTERNOONS.

Perfect Parties | 39

OUTDOOR BLISS

Cheerful lettuce ware, wicker chargers, and bamboo accents mingle among dahlias, roses, and hydrangeas to heighten the natural charm of this luncheon's grassy locale. Napkins featuring sky blue embroidery coordinate with the checkered tablecloth and plush floral pillows for a touch of elegance. Refreshing under the summer sun, Rose Water Lemonade and Chilled Peach Soup are accompanied by herbaceous yeast rolls and Smoked Salmon Pasta Salad. The sweet finale—Raspberry Panna Cotta garnished with fruit, mint, and dollops of cream—is perfectly portioned in etched coupe glasses that reprise the tabletop's floral motif.

Rose Water Lemonade
MAKES 4 TO 6 SERVINGS

2 cups sugar
2 cups water
5 cups cold water
2 cups ice, plus more for serving
2 cups fresh lemon juice
2 teaspoons rose water
Garnish: lemon slices, edible petals

1. In a saucepan over medium heat, combine sugar and 2 cups water. Bring to a boil, stirring until sugar dissolves. Let cool. Add mixture to a large pitcher, and stir in 5 cups cold water, ice, lemon juice, and rose water.
2. Fill glasses with ice. Divide lemonade between glasses. Garnish with lemon and petals, if desired.

Chilled Peach Soup
MAKES 4 TO 6 SERVINGS

3 cups peeled sliced peaches
3 cups chopped yellow tomato
1 cup finely chopped peeled seedless cucumber
¼ cup diced yellow onion
¼ cup Champagne vinegar
2 tablespoons honey
1 tablespoon kosher salt, divided
¼ cup plus 1 tablespoon olive oil, divided
1 cup torn sourdough, about ¼-inch pieces
Sour cream, to serve
Garnish: diced fresh peaches, fresh basil leaves

1. In a large bowl, combine sliced peaches, tomato, cucumber, onion, vinegar, honey, and 2 teaspoons salt. Cover and refrigerate at least 2 hours or overnight. Transfer mixture to the container of a blender; process until smooth. With the blender running, gradually add ¼ cup olive oil, in a slow and steady stream, until fully combined. Cover and refrigerate soup until ready to serve.
2. Preheat oven to 375°. Line a rimmed baking sheet with parchment paper.

3. Arrange sourdough in an even layer. Drizzle with remaining 1 tablespoon olive oil and sprinkle with remaining 1 teaspoon salt.
4. Bake until golden brown and toasted, 15 to 20 minutes.
5. Top servings of soup with toasted sourdough and serve with sour cream. Garnish with peaches and basil, if desired.

Dill–Sour Cream Rolls
MAKES 12

¼ cup warm water (105° to 110°)
1 (0.25-ounce) package active dry yeast
½ cup sour cream
¼ cup unsalted butter
¼ cup sugar
1½ teaspoons kosher salt
1 large egg, lightly beaten
2¾ cups all-purpose flour
1 cup grated Parmesan cheese, divided
1 clove garlic, minced
2 tablespoons minced fresh dill
2 tablespoons unsalted butter, melted
Garnish: chopped fresh dill

1. In the bowl of a stand mixer fitted with the paddle attachment, combine ¼ cup warm water and yeast. Let stand until mixture is foamy, about 10 minutes.
2. In a medium saucepan, heat sour cream, butter, sugar, and salt over medium-low heat, stirring constantly, until butter is melted, 3 to 4 minutes. Let cool to 110°, about 10 minutes. Add egg and sour cream mixture to yeast mixture, beating until combined.
3. Add flour, ¾ cup cheese, garlic, and dill, and beat at medium speed until well combined. Spray a large bowl with cooking spray. Place dough in bowl, turning to grease top. Cover and let

Perfect Parties | 43

rise in a warm, draft-free place (75°) until doubled in size, 1 hour to 1 hour 30 minutes.

4. Spray a 12-cup muffin pan with cooking spray.

5. Divide dough into 12 equal portions. Working with 1 portion at a time (keep remaining dough covered to keep from drying out), divide each portion into 3 pieces; roll each piece into a ball. Place 3 dough balls in each prepared muffin cup. Cover and let rise in a warm, draft-free place (75°) until doubled in size, about 30 minutes.

6. Preheat oven to 350°.

7. Bake until golden brown, about 15 minutes. Remove from oven. Brush with melted butter, and sprinkle with remaining ¼ cup cheese. Garnish with dill, if desired.

Smoked Salmon Pasta Salad with Peas and Arugula
MAKES 4 TO 6 SERVINGS

2 tablespoons plus 1 teaspoon kosher salt, divided
1 cup fresh peas
¼ cup mayonnaise
¼ cup buttermilk
1 teaspoon lemon zest
2 tablespoons fresh lemon juice
½ teaspoon coarse ground black pepper
4 cups cooked shell pasta
1 (4-ounce) package fresh baby arugula
¼ cup sliced red onion
1 tablespoon chopped fresh parsley
1 teaspoon chopped fresh dill
2 (4-ounce) hot-smoked salmon fillets
Lemon wedges, to serve
Garnish: coarse ground black pepper

1. Fill a small saucepan halfway with water and season with 2 tablespoons salt. Bring to a boil over medium-high heat. Add peas and cook until brightened in color and crisp tender, 1 to 2 minutes. Drain peas and transfer to an ice water bath to stop the cooking process; drain well and reserve.

2. In a large bowl, whisk together mayonnaise, buttermilk, lemon zest and juice, pepper, and remaining 1 teaspoon salt. Add pasta and stir until well combined. Add arugula, red onion, parsley, dill, and reserved peas, gently tossing to combine.

3. Remove skin from salmon and flake with a fork. Add to salad and gently toss to combine. Serve with lemon wedges. Garnish with pepper, if desired.

Raspberry Panna Cotta
MAKES 6 SERVINGS

¼ cup cold water
1½ teaspoons unflavored gelatin
2 cups fresh raspberries
⅓ cup sugar
2 tablespoons raspberry liqueur
1 teaspoon vanilla extract
⅛ teaspoon kosher salt
1½ cups heavy whipping cream
Garnish: sweetened whipped cream, fresh mint leaves, fresh raspberries

1. In a small bowl, stir together ¼ cup cold water and gelatin. Let stand until softened, about 5 minutes.

2. In a small saucepan, bring raspberries, sugar, raspberry liqueur, vanilla, and salt to a boil over medium-high heat. Reduce heat and simmer, stirring frequently, about 10 minutes. Transfer raspberry mixture to the container of a blender; process until smooth. Strain mixture through a very fine-mesh sieve to remove any seeds, making sure to retrieve any purée from bottom of sieve. Return raspberry mixture to saucepan; bring to a simmer over medium heat. Add gelatin mixture to raspberry mixture, stirring until gelatin dissolves. Remove from heat; add cream, stirring until well incorporated.

3. Divide mixture between 6 coupe or gelato glasses. Place glasses on a rimmed baking sheet. Refrigerate until mixture is firm, about 3 hours. Garnish with whipped cream, mint, and raspberries, if desired.

Outdoor Savvy

Throw a foolproof alfresco gathering with this advice from event planners Lisa Milko and Lydia Noble, experts in pulling off a fabulous party.

❀ **WORK WITH YOUR VENUE.** Lisa Milko of Atlanta-based company Event Perfect asks her clients to think about the capacity of their location first. "Don't crowd your crowd," she says. "Give them ample room to mingle, dance, play—whatever you have planned. By contrast, don't dwarf your group in a huge space. It will feel cold and empty. The space will set the tone for your event." In her work with Noble Events, LLC, Lydia Noble advises her clients all across the Southeast to start with what they have. "If you have violets in your yard, use that color as your starting point to build your color palette," she says.

❀ **CREATE HYDRATION STATIONS.** Whether it be water, tea, lemonade, or cocktails, have beverages readily available around the event space. For a creative touch, Lisa suggests infused water stations or ice cubes with edible flowers frozen inside. "They can be tailored to your menu or décor and will keep your guests hydrated and happy," she says. Lydia feels it's also important to offer ice scoops, glasses for different drinks, and cocktail napkins. "People hate to have to ask what to do," she says. "If you supply all their equipment, they are much more comfortable."

❀ **SERVE SMART.** Make sure your menu is suited for warm weather with lighter fare that's easy to pick up and eat while socializing. "A Mediterranean display of olives, dip, cheeses, and skewered meats is perfect," Lisa says. "Popsicles are fun, and you can make them grown-up too." You can also use decorative signage to label each food and drink item. "Keep guests informed without having to verbally explain every detail to them," Lydia says.

❀ **HIRE A COMPANY TO BUS TABLES.** "During parties, people forget that someone, usually the host, must clean up," Lydia says. To minimize distractions from conversing with guests, hire a few bussers to keep the tables tidy throughout the gathering. "They'll care for all your china, glassware, and garbage at the end of the event," she says.

❀ **EXPECT THE UNEXPECTED.** Lisa arms herself with a personalized emergency kit for every event. "It's always smart to be prepared for things you might need on-site," she says. She includes items like bug spray, pain reliever, and even candles in case a guest brings a surprise cake for a birthday. The bottom line: As a hostess, you can never be too prepared.

Mother's Day Memories

SERVE RECIPES OF THE PAST AND DECORATE WITH TIMELESS KEEPSAKES TO HONOR A SPECIAL LADY DESERVING OF ENDLESS APPRECIATION.

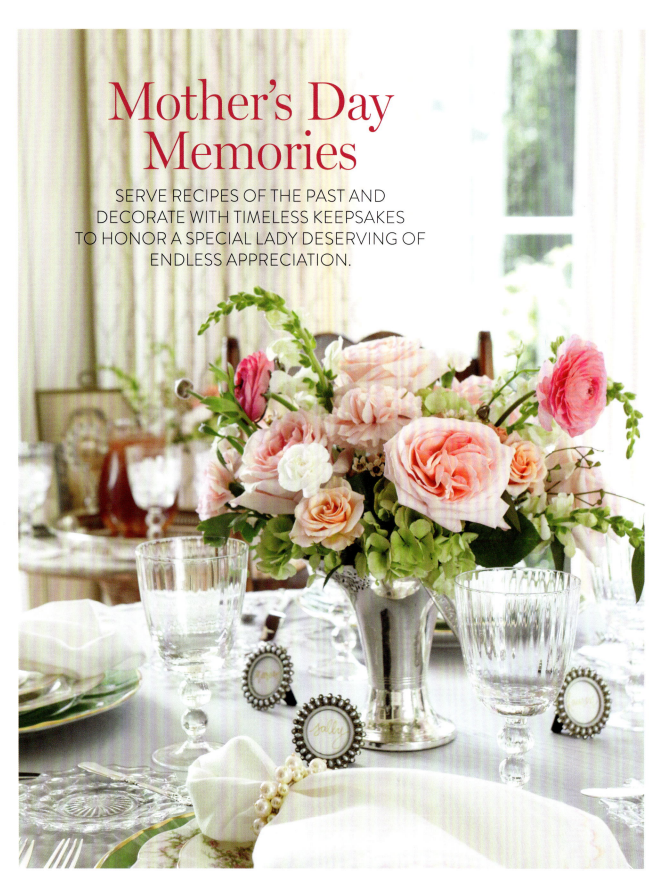

BLISSFUL TRADITION

The month of May calls for paying tribute to the women who care unconditionally, who dry tears and encourage smiles, who infuse life with laughter and love. Distinguish an exclusive seat for your family's matriarch with a silver vessel full of peachy blooms. A draping ribbon in a complementary hue enhances the arrangements of pink ranunculus, green hydrangeas, white carnations, and an array of roses. Anchored by a mint charger trimmed in gold, floral-adorned china imparts a feminine flourish paired with a lace tablecloth and delicately embroidered linens. A symbol of the pure, precious nature of a mother-daughter bond, pearl napkin rings top off the refined presentation. Miniature frames with personalized name cards keep company with handed-down flatware and cherished photographs displayed nearby.

Peach-Infused Sweet Tea
MAKES 2 QUARTS

3 fresh peaches, sliced
1 cup sugar
1 cup water
6 cups boiling water
3 iced tea bags
2 hibiscus herbal tea bags*
Garnish: fresh peach slices

1. In a medium saucepan, bring peaches, sugar, and 1 cup water to a boil over medium-high heat. Remove from heat; cover and let steep for 30 minutes.
2. Strain mixture into a 2-quart pitcher. Add 6 cups boiling water and all tea bags. Let steep for 6 minutes. Let cool completely. Serve over ice. Garnish with peaches, if desired.

*We used TAZO Passion tea.

Shrimp Toast Points
MAKES 4 SERVINGS

6 slices water chestnut
1½ teaspoons ground ginger
½ cup medium fresh shrimp, peeled and deveined
1 green onion (green part only)
2 tablespoons beaten egg
1 tablespoon cold unsalted butter
¼ teaspoon kosher salt
¼ teaspoon toasted sesame seed oil
4 thin slices white sandwich bread
4 tablespoons vegetable oil, divided
Sweet Chili Sauce (recipe follows)
Garnish: toasted sesame seeds, sliced green onion

1. In the work bowl of a food processor, place water chestnuts and ginger; pulse until finely minced. Scrape sides of bowl, and add shrimp, green onion, egg, cold butter, salt, and sesame seed oil; pulse until a paste consistency is reached with a few pieces remaining. Spread 1 tablespoon shrimp paste onto each bread slice, and cut in half diagonally.
2. In a small nonstick skillet, heat 2 tablespoons vegetable oil over medium heat. Carefully place two triangles in skillet, shrimp side down; fry until golden brown, 1½ to 2 minutes per side. Repeat with remaining 2 tablespoons vegetable oil and remaining shrimp triangles. Let drain on paper towels. Garnish with sesame seeds and green onion, if desired. Serve warm with Sweet Chili Sauce.

SWEET CHILI SAUCE
MAKES ¾ CUP

2 tablespoons water
1 tablespoon cornstarch
⅓ cup sugar
⅓ cup rice vinegar
1½ tablespoons hot chili paste*

1. In a small bowl, stir together 2 tablespoons water and cornstarch until dissolved.
2. In a small saucepan, bring sugar and vinegar to a simmer over medium heat. Simmer until sugar is dissolved, 7 to 10 minutes. Stir in chili paste and cornstarch mixture; bring to a boil. Remove from heat, and let cool completely. Refrigerate for up to 1 week.

*We used sambal oelek.

Heirloom Tomato Salad
MAKES 4 SERVINGS

4 assorted heirloom tomatoes, sliced ¼ inch thick
¼ medium red onion, thinly sliced
2 tablespoons roughly chopped fresh parsley
2 tablespoons olive oil
2 tablespoons fresh lime juice
1 tablespoon finely chopped fresh oregano
1 teaspoon sea salt
½ teaspoon ground black pepper
Garnish: finely chopped fresh oregano

1. Arrange tomato and onion slices on a large platter.
2. In a small bowl, combine parsley, oil, lime juice, oregano, salt, and pepper. Pour over tomato salad. Garnish with oregano, if desired.

Classic Chicken à la King

MAKES 6 SERVINGS

1 (10-ounce) package frozen puff pastry shells*
¼ cup unsalted butter
¾ cup diced yellow onion
¾ cup sliced carrot
1 teaspoon kosher salt
½ teaspoon ground black pepper
½ teaspoon celery salt
¼ teaspoon poultry seasoning
3 tablespoons all-purpose flour
2 cups whole milk
2 cups shredded rotisserie chicken
1 cup fresh young peas
1 cup sliced fresh mushrooms
1 (4-ounce) jar diced pimientos
Garnish: chopped fresh chives

1. Preheat oven to 425°. Line a baking sheet with parchment paper.
2. Place puff pastry shells on prepared pan. Bake for 30 minutes. Remove top of each pastry shell.
3. In a large skillet, melt butter over medium heat. Add onion, carrot, salt, pepper, celery salt, and poultry seasoning; cook until onions are translucent. Whisk in flour until smooth. Cook, whisking frequently, until flour turns a deep golden brown. Slowly add milk, stirring constantly as sauce thickens. Fold in chicken, peas, mushrooms, and pimientos.
4. Fill each puff pastry with ¾ cup chicken mixture. Garnish with chives, if desired.

*We used Pepperidge Farm.

Lemon Chiffon Cake

MAKES 1 (10-INCH) CAKE

2 cups all-purpose flour
1½ cups sugar
1 tablespoon baking powder
½ teaspoon kosher salt
½ cup vegetable oil
8 large eggs, room temperature and separated
2½ tablespoons lemon zest
¼ cup fresh lemon juice
¼ cup water
Lemon Glaze (recipe follows)
Garnish: lemon slices, lemon peel

1. Preheat oven to 325°.
2. In a large bowl, stir together flour, sugar, baking powder, and salt. In a medium bowl, whisk together oil, egg yolks, lemon zest and juice, and ¼ cup water. Fold oil mixture into flour mixture.
3. In the bowl of a stand mixer fitted with the whisk attachment, beat egg whites at high speed until stiff peaks form, about 2 minutes. Fold one-third of egg whites into batter. Gently fold in remaining egg whites. (Do not overmix.) Gently transfer batter to an ungreased 10-inch tube pan.
4. Bake until top springs back when lightly touched near center, about 1 hour. Immediately invert pan; let cool completely in pan, about 1½ hours.
5. Run a knife around edges and center of pan. Invert cake onto a wire rack. Pour Lemon Glaze over cooled cake. Garnish with lemon slices and peel, if desired.

LEMON GLAZE
MAKES 1½ CUPS

2 cups confectioners' sugar
¼ cup unsalted butter, melted
¼ cup fresh lemon juice

1. In a small bowl, whisk together all ingredients until smooth. Use immediately.

Perfect Parties | 55

Together Again

REUNITE WITH LONGTIME FRIENDS IN A GARDEN SETTING THAT'S AS SPLENDID AS THE MOMENTS YOU'LL SHARE.

FOND REMEMBRANCES

The mellifluous laughter of old companions swirls on the fresh garden air as gathered ladies enjoy lunch alfresco, swapping new stories and reminiscing over days past. A blue gingham tablecloth anchors an arrangement of florals and finery, an idyllic scene for a posh picnic. Seafoam green chargers trimmed in gold and porcelain plates bearing a royal blue lace design layer in harmony; top off the duo with an accent dish that encapsulates the enchantment of Mother Nature in full bloom. Stylized bamboo flatware and woven flower containers lend textural intrigue to the scene, while buoyant blooms steal the show: 'Café au Lait' dahlias, coral peonies, hydrangeas, cornflowers, anemones, and scabiosas.

REFRESHING FARE

As the conversation flows, indulge in a spread of flavorful bites. Cool and crispy slaw peppered with fresh jalapeño complements lettuce wraps bursting with citrusy shrimp and cilantro. Sugar snap peas sautéed in garlic and lemon round out the zesty main course, and Lemonade with Mint and Honey is the perfect chilled beverage for an afternoon outside. Topped with sliced mango, a creamy lime-and-coconut semifreddo makes a luscious endnote for this reunion of dearest pals.

Cilantro-Lime Shrimp Lettuce Wraps

MAKES 6 SERVINGS

1 tablespoon olive oil
1 cup sliced red onion
1 small yellow bell pepper, seeded and sliced
1 pound medium fresh shrimp, peeled and deveined
1½ teaspoons smoked paprika
1 teaspoon kosher salt
½ teaspoon ground cumin
¼ teaspoon ground coriander
¼ teaspoon garlic powder
¼ teaspoon ground black pepper
1 lime, juiced
2 tablespoons chopped fresh cilantro
12 butter lettuce leaves
Garnish: chopped avocado, sliced radish, chopped fresh cilantro

1. In a large saucepan, heat oil over medium-high heat. Add onion and bell pepper; cook until tender, about 5 minutes. Add shrimp, paprika, salt, cumin, coriander, garlic powder, and pepper; cook, stirring occasionally, until shrimp are pink and firm, about 5 minutes. Remove from heat; stir in lime juice. Cover and refrigerate until cooled, at least 30 minutes.

2. Stir in cilantro. Using a slotted spoon, place about 2 tablespoons shrimp mixture in center of each lettuce leaf. Garnish with avocado, radish, and cilantro, if desired. Serve immediately.

Sweet and Spicy Jalapeño Slaw

MAKES 6 SERVINGS

1 (16-ounce) bag shredded coleslaw
1 to 2 small jalapeño peppers*, seeded and thinly sliced
1 cup thinly sliced red onion
¼ cup chopped green onion
¼ cup mayonnaise
2 tablespoons confectioners' sugar
2 tablespoons Dijon mustard
1 tablespoon apple cider vinegar
1 teaspoon kosher salt
½ teaspoon ground black pepper
¼ teaspoon ground cumin
Garnish: chopped green onion

1. In a large bowl, stir together coleslaw, jalapeño, red onion, and green onion. In a small bowl, whisk together mayonnaise, confectioners' sugar, mustard, vinegar, salt, pepper, and cumin until smooth. Add dressing to coleslaw mixture, stirring to coat. Cover and refrigerate for at least 1 hour or overnight. Garnish with green onion, if desired.

*Based on heat preference.

Perfect Parties

diagonally, laying flat and making sure pieces do not overlap. (Cut to fit, if necessary.)

3. In a large saucepan, bring condensed milk and coconut milk to a boil over high heat. Reduce heat to medium; cook, stirring frequently, until thickened, about 10 minutes. Remove from heat; stir in lime zest and salt. Place saucepan in prepared ice bath. Let stand, stirring frequently, until a food thermometer inserted in mixture registers 95°, about 10 minutes.

4. In a large bowl, beat cold cream with a mixer at medium-high speed until stiff peaks form, 4 to 5 minutes. Working in batches, gently fold whipped cream into milk mixture. Pour cream mixture into prepared pan. Sprinkle with coconut, and gently press into cream mixture. Cover and freeze until firm, at least 6 hours or overnight.

5. Let stand at room temperature for 10 minutes. Invert onto a serving platter. Garnish with coconut and zest, if desired. Serve immediately.

Lemonade with Mint and Honey
MAKES ABOUT 1½ QUARTS

6 cups water, divided
½ cup wildflower honey
1 cup fresh mint leaves
1 cup fresh lemon juice
Garnish: lemon slices, fresh mint sprigs

1. In a small saucepan, bring 1 cup water and honey to a simmer over medium heat, whisking until honey is dissolved. Remove from heat; add mint leaves. Using the back of a spoon, muddle mint.
2. Transfer honey mixture to a pitcher; stir in lemon juice and remaining 5 cups water. Refrigerate until cooled, about 30 minutes. Discard mint leaves. Add ice to serve. Garnish with lemon and mint, if desired.

> **KITCHEN TIP:**
> Add gin, vodka, or silver rum for a delightful cocktail.

Lemon-Garlic Snap Peas
MAKES 6 SERVINGS

1 tablespoon olive oil
1 pound fresh sugar snap peas, trimmed
2 cloves garlic, minced
1 lemon, zested and juiced
1 teaspoon kosher salt
½ teaspoon ground black pepper
Garnish: lemon zest

1. In a large saucepan, heat oil over high heat. Add snap peas and garlic; cook, stirring frequently, until tender, about 3 minutes. Add lemon zest and juice, salt, and pepper; cook until liquid is evaporated, about 1 minute. Garnish with zest, if desired.

Coconut-Mango Semifreddo
MAKES 6 TO 8 SERVINGS

1 large ripe mango, thinly sliced
1 (14-ounce) can sweetened condensed milk
1 (13.66-ounce) can unsweetened coconut milk
1 tablespoon lime zest
¼ teaspoon kosher salt
1½ cups heavy whipping cream, chilled
½ cup sweetened flaked coconut, toasted
Garnish: toasted flaked coconut, lime zest

1. Line an 8½x4½-inch loaf pan with parchment paper, letting excess extend over sides of pan. In a large bowl, prepare an ice bath.
2. In prepared pan, arrange mango slices

Sipping Pretty

Top off a chilled beverage with a simple garnish that calls to mind golden rays of sunshine.

1. Using a channel knife, pare ribbons of peel lengthwise from a fresh lemon, leaving the white pith intact and allowing a small space between each cut for a striped effect.

2. Once you've worked your way around the entire lemon, lay it on a cutting board and slice crosswise into rounds.

3. Make a slit at one edge of each round to allow it to perch neatly on the rim of a glass.

Flowers & Finery

GATHER GIRLFRIENDS FOR A FLORAL-INFUSED LUNCHEON, TAKING CUES FROM BUDDING MUSES THAT REFLECT CORDIAL RELATIONSHIPS FLOURISHING IN TANDEM.

BEVY OF BLOOMS

An eye-catching floral wallpaper sets the scene for an ambience that captures the elegance of a traditional indoor tea party while also bringing in the beauty of the outdoors. Almost as if they're blooming upward from the table, a profusion of tulips, sweetheart roses, peonies, 'Butterfly' ranunculus, carnations, variegated pittosporum, and seeded eucalyptus cascades down its center. This striking runner is interspersed with vintage birdcages and vases in varied heights bearing even more blossoms that add depth and distinction to the vivid display. As guests take their seats, you can set taller vessels aside for ease of conversation.

Vidalia Onion-Bacon Tart
MAKES 1 (11-INCH) TART

1 (14.1-ounce) package refrigerated piecrusts, room temperature
8 slices thick-cut bacon, chopped
1½ cups thinly sliced Vidalia onion
1 teaspoon sugar
6 large eggs
1½ cups heavy cream
2 tablespoons Dijon mustard
1 tablespoon chopped fresh thyme
½ teaspoon kosher salt
¼ teaspoon ground nutmeg
¼ teaspoon ground black pepper
½ cup shredded Parmesan cheese
Garnish: fresh thyme leaves

1. Preheat oven to 375°.
2. On a lightly floured surface, unroll 1 piecrust. Lightly brush with water. Unroll remaining piecrust, and place on top. Roll into a 12-inch circle. Transfer to an 11-inch removable-bottom tart pan, pressing into bottom and up sides. Trim edges. Lightly cover with parchment paper, and add pie weights.
3. Bake until light golden brown, 12 to 15 minutes. Remove paper and weights. Let cool slightly.
4. In a large saucepan, cook bacon over medium-high heat, stirring occasionally, until crispy, about 15 minutes. Using a slotted spoon, remove bacon, and let drain on paper towels. Add onion to pan. Reduce heat to medium, and cook, stirring occasionally, until tender, about 5 minutes. Stir in sugar, and cook until golden brown, about 5 minutes. Using a slotted spoon, remove onion mixture, and let drain on paper towels.
5. In a large bowl, whisk together eggs, cream, mustard, thyme, salt, nutmeg, and pepper until smooth. Stir in half of bacon and half of onion mixture. Pour into prepared crust. Sprinkle with cheese, remaining bacon, and remaining onion mixture.
6. Bake until puffed and golden brown, about 25 minutes. Let cool slightly. Garnish with thyme, if desired. Serve warm or at room temperature.

Asparagus-Avocado Bisque
MAKES 6 TO 8 SERVINGS

1 tablespoon olive oil
1 bunch asparagus, trimmed and cut into 1-inch pieces
¾ teaspoon kosher salt, divided
2½ cups vegetable broth
1 cup heavy whipping cream
2 ripe avocados, cubed
1 tablespoon chopped fresh chives
1 teaspoon fresh lemon juice
¼ teaspoon ground white pepper
Garnish: olive oil

1. In a medium Dutch oven, heat oil over medium-high heat. Add asparagus and ¼ teaspoon salt; cook, stirring occasionally, for about 3 minutes. Add broth, and bring to a boil over medium-high heat; reduce heat, and simmer, stirring occasionally, until tender, about 5 minutes. Reserve ⅓ cup asparagus mixture.
2. In the container of a blender, place remaining asparagus mixture, cream, avocado, chives, lemon juice, pepper, and remaining ½ teaspoon salt; process until smooth.
3. Return soup to Dutch oven, and cook until heated through. Top with reserved ⅓ cup asparagus mixture and garnish with oil, if desired.

KITCHEN TIP:
This can be served chilled.

Herb Butter Smashed Peas
MAKES 6 TO 8 SERVINGS

½ cup unsalted butter
4 cups shelled fresh English peas
2 cups vegetable broth
1 cup chopped green onion
4 teaspoons kosher salt
½ teaspoon ground black pepper
½ cup chopped fresh parsley
¼ cup chopped fresh chives
2 lemons, zested
Garnish: lemon zest, chopped fresh parsley

1. In a small Dutch oven, melt butter over medium heat. Add peas, broth, green onion, salt, and pepper; cook, stirring occasionally, until vegetables are tender, 15 to 20 minutes. Using the back of a spoon, mash half of peas. Remove from heat; stir in parsley, chives, and zest. Garnish with zest and parsley, if desired.

Lemon-Lavender Sablés
MAKES ABOUT 18 COOKIES

1 cup granulated sugar
3 teaspoons lightly packed lemon zest, divided
1½ teaspoons culinary lavender
1 vanilla bean, split lengthwise, seeds scraped, reserved, and divided
1 cup unsalted butter, softened
⅓ cup confectioners' sugar
1 teaspoon kosher salt
1 large egg yolk
2¼ cups all-purpose flour
½ cup blanched almond meal

1. In the work bowl of a food processor, pulse granulated sugar, 1 teaspoon lemon zest, lavender, and half of vanilla bean seeds until lavender is finely ground and mixture is combined. Place lavender sugar in a medium bowl.
2. In the bowl of a stand mixer fitted with paddle attachment, beat butter at medium-low speed until creamy, about 1 minute. Add ¼ cup lavender sugar, confectioners' sugar, and salt, beating until smooth, about 1 minute. Add egg yolk, remaining 2 teaspoons lemon zest, and remaining half of vanilla bean seeds, beating until combined, about 1 minute.
3. In a medium bowl, whisk together flour and almond meal. Add flour mixture to butter mixture in two additions, beating until just combined.
4. Place dough between two large pieces of parchment paper, and roll to ½-inch thickness. Refrigerate dough between parchment until set, about 1 hour.
5. Preheat oven to 325°. Line 2 baking sheets with parchment paper.
6. Using a 2⅛-inch round fluted cutter dipped in flour, cut dough, and place on prepared pans at least 1 inch apart. Reroll dough scraps between parchment as necessary; freeze until set, about 5 minutes, before cutting dough again.
7. Bake until bottom edges turn golden, 16 to 20 minutes. Let cool on pan for 1 minute.
8. Place remaining lavender sugar on a large plate and, using a spatula, place cookies a few at a time in sugar, covering tops and sides. Place on a wire rack to let cool completely.

Floral Fanfare

The splendor of lush foliage and flora inspires this blossom-bordered menu artfully folded into a handheld fan—perfect for seated occasions that range from casual garden parties to sophisticated evening soirées.

1. On a flat surface, turn the menu printed side down and fold the long edge once.

2. Turn the menu printed side up and repeat fold. Continue flipping and folding accordion style until you reach the opposite edge, making sure the last fold matches the first in appearance.

3. Pinch the bottom of the menu and fold it up about 2 inches.

4. Tie a ribbon around the fold to secure.

Lunch in the Garden

FINE WEATHER AND PRISMATIC FLORA SET A PICTURESQUE SCENE FOR A MIDDAY REPAST.

VERDANT OASIS

Lured by the aroma of fresh flowers along with the melody of buzzing bees and twittering birds, gathered guests will want to stroll amid the roses all afternoon long. While all of Mother Nature may seem hard at work, relax and enjoy the view at your own pace while catching up with friends.

BRIGHT DETAILS
Take cues from the vibrant, sunny surrounds to set the table for this laid-back affair, incorporating yellows and pinks that echo the nearby blooms. An ice-cold glass of Citrus Mint Sweet Tea complements light, delicious fare—from sweet and savory pastry bundles to petite lavender-glazed Bundt cakes.

Citrus Mint Sweet Tea
MAKES 1½ GALLONS

12 cups water, divided
1½ cups sugar
4 family-size tea bags
¾ cup fresh grapefruit juice
¾ cup fresh orange juice (from about 2 oranges)
½ cup fresh lemon juice (from about 3 lemons)
3 sprigs fresh mint

1. In a medium saucepan, bring 4 cups water and sugar to a boil over medium-high heat; boil for 1 minute. Remove from heat, and pour into a pitcher.
2. In a large saucepan, bring remaining 8 cups water to a boil over medium-high heat; add tea bags. Let steep for at least 10 minutes before removing tea bags.
3. Using a fine-mesh sieve, strain fruit juices into pitcher; add hot brewed tea. Add mint, and let cool to room temperature. Remove mint sprigs; refrigerate until chilled.

Shaved Spring Salad
MAKES ABOUT 8 SERVINGS

1 (5-ounce) bag fresh spring lettuce mix
1 (12-ounce) bag rainbow carrots, shaved
6 to 8 spears asparagus, shaved
6 radishes, shaved
Honey Mustard–Poppy Seed Dressing (recipe follows)

1. In a large bowl, toss together lettuces, carrot, asparagus, and radish. Refrigerate until ready to serve. Just before serving, drizzle with Honey Mustard–Poppy Seed Dressing.

HONEY MUSTARD–POPPY SEED DRESSING
MAKES ABOUT 1½ CUPS

⅔ cup light mayonnaise
¼ cup sugar
1½ tablespoons Dijon mustard
1 tablespoon white wine vinegar
1 tablespoon extra-virgin olive oil
1 tablespoon honey
2 teaspoons poppy seeds

1. In a jar with a tight-fitting lid, place all ingredients; shake to combine. Refrigerate until ready to serve.

Fig, Ham, and Asparagus Pastry Bundles
MAKES 8

½ cup whole-milk ricotta cheese
1 tablespoon fig preserves
¼ teaspoon kosher salt
¼ teaspoon ground black pepper
1 (17.3-ounce) package frozen puff pastry, thawed
1 large egg
1 tablespoon milk
1 small bunch fresh asparagus, trimmed and peeled
16 slices Black Forest deli ham

1. Preheat oven to 425°. Line a rimmed sheet pan with parchment paper.
2. In a small bowl, combine ricotta, fig preserves, salt, and pepper.
3. On a lightly floured surface, gently roll one pastry sheet to flatten seams. Cut into 4 squares. Prick center of each square with a fork about three times. Repeat with remaining pastry sheet. In a small bowl, whisk together egg and milk. Brush squares with egg wash. Rotate squares to create a diamond shape.
4. Spread about 1 tablespoon ricotta mixture down center of each diamond, beginning and ending about 1 inch from points. Place 3 to 4 asparagus spears on two slices of ham. Wrap asparagus inside ham, and place on ricotta mixture. Roll up pastry, and place on prepared pan. Brush with egg wash.
5. Bake until golden brown and puffed, about 15 minutes. Serve warm.

Mini Almond Bundt Cakes with Lavender Glaze
MAKES 12

Cakes:
2½ cups granulated sugar
2 large eggs, room temperature
1½ cups whole milk, room temperature
2 teaspoons almond extract
2½ cups all-purpose flour
1 teaspoon baking powder
½ cup unsalted butter, melted

Glaze:
1½ cups confectioners' sugar
¼ cup whole milk
1 teaspoon dried lavender buds

1. Preheat oven to 350°. Generously spray 2 (6-well) miniature Bundt cake pans with baking spray with flour.
2. For cakes: In the bowl of a stand mixer fitted with the paddle attachment, beat granulated sugar and eggs at medium speed until well combined and pale yellow. Beat in milk and almond extract.
3. In a medium bowl, whisk together flour and baking powder. With mixer on low speed, gradually add flour mixture to sugar mixture, beating until well combined, stopping to scrape sides of bowl. Gradually add melted butter, beating until combined. Pour batter into prepared pans.
4. Bake until a wooden pick inserted near center comes out clean, 35 to 40 minutes. Let cool in pans for 10 minutes. Remove from pans, and let cool completely on wire racks before glazing.
5. For glaze: In a small bowl, whisk together confectioners' sugar, milk, and lavender. Pour about 1 tablespoon glaze over each cake. Store cakes in an airtight container.

Chilled to Perfection

Bring fresh flair to your event by fashioning a stylish ice block filled with bright citrus and herbs, ideal for keeping a delicious beverage cool.

1. To create a 2-inch block, start with two flat-bottomed circular containers (we used glass) varying in height; one should be 2 inches taller and 4 inches smaller in diameter than the other.

2. Fill half of the larger diameter container with water and then set the smaller one inside it, taping it at the top edges to secure it from bobbling.

3. Slice citrus fruits, the more colorful the better, and select full leaves from herbs like mint and basil. Position the fruit and herbs in the water in the gap between the two containers, using long kitchen tongs to situate them so they will be visible through the ice.

4. Carefully place the containers in the freezer until the water is completely frozen.

5. Just before serving, put the fused containers in the sink for about 15 minutes; a slight melt will loosen the ice block, allowing for easier removal.

6. Detach the inner container first and then remove the outer, leaving only the formed ice block.

7. Set the block on any waterproof high-lip dish to account for melting, and it's ready to chill the bottled beverage of your choice. Once the bottle is in place, fill any remaining space with cubed ice for optimal cooling. Enjoy!

Perfect Parties | 87

3

Love Is in the Air

REJOICE IN HEARTFELT BONDS AT FÊTES COMMEMORATING BLUSHING BRIDES, NEWLYWEDS, AND COUPLES WHO HAVE STOOD THE TEST OF TIME.

Enchanted Evening

INDULGE IN A SUMPTUOUS SUPPER FOR TWO, WHERE LOVELY VINTAGE DETAILS NOD TO A ROMANCE THAT GROWS GREATER WITH AGE.

OLD-FASHIONED CHARM

A soft, dreamy palette embodies the enduring elegance of days gone by to create an enchanting scene on this occasion made for doting on your special someone. A linen cloth covered in a faded floral print serves as a beautiful backdrop for an organic runner composed of eucalyptus swags interspersed with pink stock, ivory tea roses, and antique pearls. The display culminates at the table's center in an arrangement teeming with garden roses, hydrangeas, tulips, ranunculus, and dusty miller. Heirloom silver and cream-colored china trimmed in motifs of intricate lace and pastel blossoms enhance the quaint aesthetic, and vintage Valentine's Day cards and packages wrapped with affection add fanciful touches to the sentimental affair. A sideboard bedecked with coordinating accents continues the ambience, presenting flowers and frills atop a gilded tray. Treasured mementos are given pride of place, while a miniature book filled with tender missives awaits an admirer.

SPREAD TO SAVOR

Begin the evening with a crisp salad as vibrant as the connection you hold dear. Short ribs braised with red wine, garlic, and thyme make for a hearty main course bolstered by a flavorful sauce. Egg noodles coated in nutty browned butter and fresh herbs are a satisfying side, while lemony asparagus sprinkled with Parmesan and walnuts provides a lighter counterpart. Strawberry Pie Love Letters deliver a fitting finale, topped by berries and sweetened whipped cream. Cap the night with decadent White Russian Coffee as you reminisce on your shared past and dream about the future.

Orange and Radicchio Salad

MAKES 2 SERVINGS

2½ tablespoons orange juice
1 tablespoon white balsamic vinegar
½ tablespoon orange marmalade
½ teaspoon orange zest
¼ teaspoon kosher salt
¼ teaspoon ground black pepper
2 tablespoons olive oil
1 blood orange, peeled, sliced into ¼-inch rounds, and seeds removed
1 Cara Cara navel orange, peeled, sliced into ¼-inch rounds, and seeds removed
½ head radicchio, leaves torn
½ cup thinly sliced fennel
Garnish: fennel fronds

1. In a small bowl, whisk together orange juice, vinegar, marmalade, zest, salt, and pepper. Slowly whisk in oil in a slow stream. Cover and refrigerate for up to 1 week.
2. Arrange oranges, radicchio, and fennel on 2 salad plates. Drizzle with orange vinaigrette. Garnish with fennel fronds, if desired.

Wine-Braised Short Ribs

MAKES 2 SERVINGS

4 beef short ribs, cut 2 inches thick (about 2 pounds)
1½ teaspoons kosher salt
1 teaspoon ground black pepper
8 to 10 fresh thyme sprigs
4 fresh rosemary sprigs
2 tablespoons canola oil
1 tablespoon all-purpose flour
2 cups beef broth
1 cup red wine
1 small yellow onion, quartered
3 cloves garlic
1 tablespoon lemon juice
4 tablespoons unsalted butter
Garnish: fresh thyme

1. Preheat oven to 325°.
2. Sprinkle short ribs with salt and pepper. Let sit at room temperature for 30 minutes. Tie thyme and rosemary sprigs together with kitchen twine.
3. In a medium ovenproof skillet, heat oil over medium-high heat. Add short ribs, and cook until browned, 1 to 2 minutes on each side. Remove short ribs from pan and set aside. Reduce heat to medium and add flour. Cook, stirring constantly, until flour is fragrant, about 2 to 3 minutes. Whisk in broth and wine. Add short ribs to pan with onion, garlic, and herb bundle. Cover and bake until meat is very tender, about 1 hour and 30 minutes to 2 hours.
4. Remove short ribs from pan; set aside. Discard onion, garlic, and herb bundle.
5. Bring remaining sauce in pan to a boil over medium-high heat. Add lemon juice. Cook, whisking constantly, until sauce is reduced by two-thirds and is thickened, about 20 to 25 minutes. Whisk

until butter turns a medium-brown color and has a nutty aroma, about 10 minutes.
3. Discard sage sprig, and add noodles back to pan. Add chives, thyme, salt, and pepper, tossing to coat.
4. Divide noodles between serving plates; top with Parmesan and toasted pine nuts.

Asparagus with Lemon and Parmesan
MAKES 2 SERVINGS

1 tablespoon lemon juice
1 tablespoon extra-virgin olive oil
¼ teaspoon kosher salt
¼ teaspoon ground black pepper
½ pound asparagus, trimmed
2 tablespoons grated Parmesan cheese
2 tablespoons chopped walnuts

1. Preheat oven to 400°.
2. In a small bowl, whisk together lemon juice, oil, salt, and pepper.
3. On a rimmed baking sheet, toss asparagus in lemon juice mixture until well coated. Arrange asparagus on pan in a single layer. Bake until asparagus are crisp-tender and starting to brown, about 5 minutes. Sprinkle with Parmesan and walnuts, and bake for 2 minutes more. Serve immediately.

White Russian Coffee
MAKES 1 SERVING

1 ounce vanilla vodka
2 ounces Kahlúa
4 ounces hot strong-brewed coffee
2 ounces heavy whipping cream
1 tablespoon Sweet Whipped Cream, to serve (recipe follows)
Garnish: milk chocolate curls

1. In an 8-ounce mug, stir together vodka, Kahlúa, coffee, and heavy whipping cream. Serve with Sweet Whipped Cream, and garnish with chocolate curls, if desired.

in butter until fully incorporated.
6. Arrange short ribs on serving plate and serve with pan sauce. Garnish with fresh thyme, if desired.

Browned Butter–Herb Noodles
MAKES 2 SERVINGS

2 cups wide egg noodles
½ cup unsalted butter
1 fresh sage sprig
2 teaspoons thinly sliced fresh chives
1 teaspoon chopped fresh thyme
½ teaspoon kosher salt
¼ teaspoon ground black pepper
2 tablespoons shaved Parmesan cheese
1 tablespoon pine nuts, toasted

1. Cook noodles according to package directions. Rinse under cold water and drain.
2. In a 10-inch skillet, melt butter over medium heat. Add sage sprig and cook

SWEET WHIPPED CREAM
MAKES ½ CUP

¼ cup heavy whipping cream
2 teaspoons granulated sugar
¼ teaspoon clear vanilla extract

1. In a chilled medium bowl and using chilled beaters, beat cream, sugar, and vanilla with a mixer at medium-high speed until medium peaks form. Serve immediately.

Strawberry Pie Love Letters
MAKES 2

½ (14.1-ounce) package refrigerated piecrusts
¼ cup thinly sliced fresh strawberries
1 tablespoon seedless strawberry preserves
½ teaspoon cornstarch
1 tablespoon whole milk
½ teaspoon sparkling sugar
Sweetened whipped cream, to serve
Garnish: thinly sliced strawberries

1. Preheat oven to 375°. Line a rimmed baking sheet with parchment paper. Spray 2 (4-inch) squares of foil with cooking spray.
2. On a lightly floured surface, roll out dough. Using a fluted pastry cutter, cut a 6-inch square from dough. Cut 3 (¾-inch) hearts from excess dough. Roll remaining dough scraps into ⅛-inch thickness and repeat procedure.
3. For each pie, arrange dough into a diamond shape. In a small bowl, gently toss together strawberries, preserves, and cornstarch. Spoon half of strawberry mixture into the center of dough. Fold bottom point over strawberry mixture; fold right and left points toward the center. Brush dough with milk. Place 1 heart in center where points meet and 1 on each side. Leave top point unfolded. Sprinkle dough with ¼ teaspoon sugar. Place on prepared pan.
4. Bake until pastry is golden brown, about 20 minutes. Cover the unfolded points loosely with prepared foil squares, coated side down, after 10 minutes to prevent overbrowning, if necessary. Let cool completely.
5. Serve with whipped cream. Garnish with strawberries, if desired.

Perfect Parties

Sweet as Honey

GATHER IN A LUXURIOUS OUTDOOR LOCALE FOR A BRIDAL SHOWER INSPIRED BY NATURE'S GOLDEN ELIXIR.

BELOVED OCCASION

The heady scents of fragrant petals swirl through the air as well-wishers celebrate a bride's upcoming nuptial bliss at a honeymoon-themed affair. A fern pattern on the tablecloth accentuates the verdant setting where invitees partake of a honey-infused spread evoking the sweetness of love. Grounding the lush atmosphere, wicker detailing on chairs, vases, and napkin rings contrasts with soft elements like ruffled napkins and a pintucked place mat. Placed near touches of gold and silver in a framed menu and flatware, crisp white plates brighten the display that greets all who convene for this felicitous moment.

Perfect Parties | 101

Honeysuckle Sweet Tea
MAKES ABOUT 2 QUARTS

8 cups water, divided
3 tablespoons honeysuckle tea*, tied in cheesecloth with twine
⅔ cup honey
1 tablespoon fresh lemon juice
Garnish: thinly sliced lemons

1. In a medium saucepan, bring 6 cups water to a boil over medium heat. Once boiling, remove from heat and add tea bundle; cover and let steep for 20 minutes. Remove tea bundle and stir in honey and lemon juice. Refrigerate until chilled, about 1 hour. Just before serving, add remaining 2 cups water and pour into a pitcher filled with ice. Garnish with lemon, if desired.

*We used Harney & Sons Honeysuckle Tea.

Melon Salad with Vanilla-Honey Dressing
MAKES 6 SERVINGS

2 cups (1-inch) watermelon balls
2 cups (1-inch) cantaloupe balls
2 cups (1-inch) honeydew balls
1 tablespoon chopped fresh mint
2 tablespoons honey
1½ tablespoons lime zest
1 teaspoon vanilla bean paste
Garnish: fresh mint leaves

1. In a large bowl, combine watermelon, cantaloupe, honeydew, and chopped mint.
2. In a small bowl, combine honey, lime zest, and vanilla bean paste. Pour over watermelon mixture, gently tossing until combined. Garnish with mint, if desired.

Gingered Chicken Skewers
MAKES 6

½ cup honey, divided
¼ cup soy sauce
2 tablespoons fresh lemon juice
1 tablespoon minced fresh ginger
1 teaspoon dark sesame oil
1 teaspoon Worcestershire sauce
4 cloves garlic, minced
1 pound skinless boneless chicken breasts, cut into 1-inch pieces
¼ pound fresh asparagus, trimmed and cut into 1½-inch pieces
1 tablespoon water
1 small yellow bell pepper, seeded and cut into 1-inch pieces
Fresh Bibb lettuce leaves
Garnish: finely chopped fresh chives

1. In a small bowl, whisk together ¼ cup honey, soy sauce, lemon juice, ginger, oil, Worcestershire, and garlic.
2. Pour half of honey mixture into a resealable plastic bag. Add chicken and refrigerate for at least 1 hour or up to overnight. Before cooking, add remaining ¼ cup honey to remaining honey mixture. Cover and refrigerate, reserving until ready to use.
3. In a medium microwave-safe bowl, combine asparagus and 1 tablespoon water. Cover with plastic wrap and microwave on high until asparagus is crisp-tender, 1 to 2 minutes (do not overcook). Let cool completely.
4. Remove chicken from bag, discarding marinade. Assemble skewers by threading chicken, steamed asparagus, and bell pepper as desired. Strain reserved honey mixture through a fine-mesh sieve, reserving marinade and discarding solids.
5. In a small saucepan, bring strained honey mixture to a low simmer over medium heat. Remove from heat; cover, and set aside while grilling the skewers.
6. Heat a cast-iron grill pan over medium-high heat. Cook skewers,

turning occasionally, until grill marks appear and chicken is cooked through, 7 to 8 minutes. Arrange skewers on a platter lined with lettuce leaves. Serve warm with honey sauce. Garnish with chives, if desired.

Lemon-Honey Cheesecake Bars

MAKES 24

- 2 cups finely crushed graham cracker crumbs
- 5 tablespoons unsalted butter, melted
- 2 tablespoons granulated sugar
- ½ teaspoon kosher salt, divided
- ¼ cup honey
- 1 tablespoon lemon zest
- 3 (8-ounce) packages cream cheese, room temperature
- ¾ cup firmly packed light brown sugar
- 3 tablespoons all-purpose flour
- 3 large eggs, room temperature
- ¾ cup sour cream, room temperature
- Garnish: edible micro sun daisies*

1. Preheat oven to 350°. Spray a 13x9-inch baking pan with cooking spray; line with foil, letting excess extend over sides.
2. In a large bowl, stir together graham cracker crumbs, melted butter, granulated sugar, and ¼ teaspoon salt until well combined. Using a straight-sided measuring cup, press into bottom of prepared pan.
3. Bake until set and fragrant, 8 to 10 minutes. Let cool on a wire rack for 30 minutes. Wrap bottom and sides of pan in a double layer of heavy-duty foil. Reduce oven temperature to 325°.
4. In a small saucepan, bring honey and lemon zest to a boil over medium heat, stirring occasionally, about 10 to 15 minutes. Remove from heat; keep warm (see Kitchen Tip).
5. In the bowl of a stand mixer fitted with the paddle attachment, beat cream cheese at medium speed until smooth and creamy, 1 to 2 minutes, stopping to scrape sides of bowl. Add brown sugar, warm honey mixture, flour, and remaining ¼ teaspoon salt; beat at medium speed until combined. Add eggs, one at a time, beating just until combined after each addition, stopping to scrape sides of bowl. Add sour cream, beat until well combined, 1 to 2 minutes, stopping to scrape sides of bowl. Pour mixture onto prepared crust.
6. Place baking pan in a large roasting pan. Place roasting pan in oven and add water to come up 1 inch on the outside of baking pan.
7. Bake until edges are set, top looks dry, center is almost set, and an instant-read thermometer inserted in center registers 150°, 35 to 40 minutes.
8. Let cool in pan on a wire rack for 1 hour and 30 minutes to 2 hours. Refrigerate in pan overnight, loosely covering with foil only when completely cool to prevent condensation from forming on top of cheesecake. Using excess foil as handles, carefully remove from pan and transfer to a cutting board. Trim edges from cheesecake. Cut into 2-inch squares. Just before serving, garnish with micro sun daisies, if desired.

*We used Gourmet Sweet Botanicals Micro Flowers Edible Micro Sun Daisy.

KITCHEN TIP:
The honey mixture will not incorporate into the cheesecake mixture if allowed to cool. If the honey mixture becomes too thick or too cool, place in a microwave-safe bowl and heat in 10-second intervals until liquid.

Something Blue

BORROW THE SIGNATURE HUE OF A WEDDING-DAY TOKEN
TO FASHION A TABLEAU BEFITTING BRIDAL BLISS.

ALL FOR LOVE

Before they walk down the aisle one by one, bridesmaids join their betrothed friend for a special luncheon. A palette of blue and white paints the scene, artfully arranged for dear companions to share cherished memories and make lasting new ones. As a nod to her veil and wedding-day bouquet, a tulle bow and lovely nosegay distinguish the bride's chair. Petite vessels brimming with white spray roses and blue delphinium serve as place cards for honored guests. Heirloom linens and ginger jars anchor the table, which is set for a spread of Chicken Salad Lettuce Cups, homemade Cheese Wafers, Mini Mushroom Tarts, and Rhubarb Pavlovas. Toast the occasion with a bubbly sipper, and present each friend with a thoughtful gift such as a meaningful silver charm.

Chicken Salad Lettuce Cups
MAKES 6 SERVINGS

4 cups shredded rotisserie chicken
1 apple, cored and diced
½ cup mayonnaise
½ cup sour cream
¼ cup smoked almonds, chopped
2 tablespoons minced fresh tarragon
1 tablespoon Dijon mustard
1 teaspoon minced garlic
½ teaspoon ground black pepper
½ teaspoon smoked paprika
½ teaspoon celery salt
2 small heads butter lettuce, leaves separated
Garnish: chopped fresh tarragon

1. In a large bowl, combine chicken, apple, mayonnaise, sour cream, almonds, tarragon, mustard, garlic, pepper, paprika, and celery salt. Refrigerate for at least 4 hours.
2. Spoon chicken salad into lettuce cups. Garnish with tarragon, if desired.

Cheese Wafers
MAKES ABOUT 24

1 cup all-purpose flour
½ cup shredded mild Cheddar cheese
½ cup shredded Monterey Jack cheese with peppers
⅓ cup cold unsalted butter, cubed
1 teaspoon kosher salt
¼ teaspoon ground black pepper
¼ teaspoon ground red pepper
¼ teaspoon smoked paprika
2 tablespoons whole milk

1. In the work bowl of a food processor, place flour, cheeses, cold butter, salt, black pepper, red pepper, and paprika; pulse until combined. With processor running, add milk in a slow, steady stream until a dough forms. Turn out dough onto a piece of plastic wrap. Shape dough into a log, twisting ends to create a tight roll. Freeze until solid.
2. Preheat oven to 350°. Line 2 baking sheets with parchment paper.
3. Slice log into ¼-inch-thick rounds, and place on prepared pans.
4. Bake until lightly browned, 18 to 20 minutes. Let cool completely.

Mini Mushroom Tarts
MAKES 8

2 tablespoons unsalted butter
2 (4-ounce) packages sliced gourmet blend mushrooms
¼ cup minced fresh parsley
1 clove garlic, minced
1 cup grated Gruyère cheese
1 large egg
1 teaspoon ground black pepper
½ teaspoon kosher salt
1 (8-ounce) box frozen mini pastry shells*, thawed
Garnish: fresh parsley leaves

1. Preheat oven to 350°.
2. In a large sauté pan, melt butter over medium heat. Add mushrooms, parsley, and garlic; cook until softened. Remove from heat; stir in cheese, egg, pepper, and salt. Divide filling among pastry shells.
3. Bake for 20 minutes. Garnish with parsley, if desired.

*We used VIP Pastry Shells.

Rhubarb Pavlovas
MAKES 6

3 large egg whites
⅛ teaspoon cream of tartar
¾ cup sugar
Rhubarb Compote (recipe follows)

1. Preheat oven to 250°. Line a baking sheet with parchment paper. Using a pencil, draw 6 (3-inch) circles on parchment; turn parchment over.
2. In the bowl of a stand mixer fitted with the whisk attachment, beat egg whites

and cream of tartar at medium speed until foamy. Add sugar, 1 tablespoon at a time, beating until stiff peaks form. Spoon mixture onto drawn circles on parchment paper.
3. Bake for 1 hour. Turn oven off, and let meringues stand in oven with door closed for 8 hours.
4. Spoon Rhubarb Compote into center of each pavlova. Serve immediately.

RHUBARB COMPOTE
MAKES 3 CUPS

6 cups chopped rhubarb
1 cup sugar
¼ teaspoon vanilla bean paste
⅛ teaspoon ground ginger

1. In a large saucepan, stir together rhubarb and sugar. Let stand at room temperature until rhubarb releases some of its liquid, about 10 minutes.
2. Bring rhubarb mixture to a boil over medium-high heat, stirring occasionally. Reduce heat; simmer, stirring occasionally, until rhubarb has broken down but some whole pieces remain, about 5 minutes. Remove from heat; stir in vanilla bean paste and ginger. Let cool completely before using.

Strawberry Bellinis
MAKES 6

2 cups sliced fresh strawberries
1 cup water
2 tablespoons sugar
1 (750-milliliter) bottle chilled prosecco
Garnish: fresh strawberry slices

1. In a medium saucepan, bring strawberries, 1 cup water, and sugar to a boil over medium-high heat. Remove from heat, and let stand for 30 minutes. Strain through a fine-mesh sieve, and let cool completely.
2. Pour about 2 tablespoons strawberry syrup into each serving glass. Fill with prosecco. Garnish with strawberries, if desired.

Thoughtful Gifting

From jazzy embellishments to classic accoutrements, wrap presents sure to make a fabulous first impression on any recipient year-round.

❀ **COORDINATE THE LOOK.** With such a spectacular array of wrapping paper widely available today, it's easier than ever to find a color or motif to suit your taste. Consider choosing a paper—or several in complementary designs—that tastefully coordinates with your tablescape and décor for the occasion at hand.

❀ **STAY EVER PREPARED.** Keep a supply of high-quality ribbon in myriad sizes, shades, and textures so you are always ready. Whether tied in a delicate knot or fashioned into an extravagant bow, ribbon spruces up any gift in a pinch. Wired varieties are wonderful for big, impressive displays; thin satin strands are ideal for petite parcels; strips of lace and crochet trimmings lend graceful texture.

❀ **CHANNEL YOUR CREATIVITY.** Presents finished with layered touches always elicit oohs and aahs. Pull from the pattern or tint of your gift wrap when selecting special baubles to affix to a package. For instance, we drew from the powder blue juniper berries depicted on a striped botanical paper when selecting treasured Wedgwood ornaments. The stunning topper doubles as a token the recipient will enjoy for years to come. Versatile craft-store finds, like faux pearls and press-on flowers, make for effortless enhancements.

❀ **FINISH WITH FRAGRANCE.** Nestled into a bow or fastened to a gift tag, fresh herbs add to the delight. Sturdy sprigs of rosemary and lavender as well as flowers with hardy stems are ideal for bestowing an invigorating aroma, further illustrating how much heart and thoughtfulness went into your special gift.

Perfect Parties | 115

Soirée for Sweethearts

ORCHESTRATE A HEARTWARMING GET-TOGETHER FOR FAMILY AND FRIENDS TO HONOR A BELOVED PAIR'S GOLDEN ANNIVERSARY.

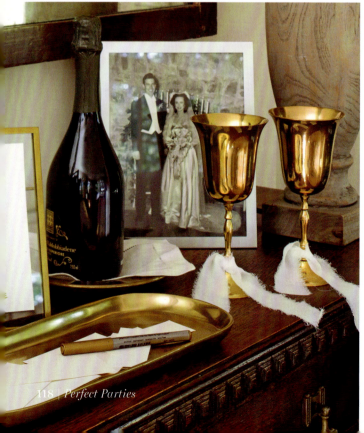

LASTING LOVE

A miscellany of lustrous accents sets the tone for an evening centered around a special duo's 50-year marriage. The shimmer of a striped ecru linen underlines a parade of golden décor, from glass dinnerware etched with an exquisite filigree-style border to knotted napkin rings made of sparkling gold rope. Dappled votives and pillar candles festooned with decorative swirling vines further the tableau's warm glow. Nestled in a gilded vessel, an ethereal fusion of white roses, lilies, and hypericum berries, interspersed with sprays of seeded eucalyptus and dusty miller, crowns the table. Those partaking in the revelry will savor a lineup of delectable fare, such as pickled shrimp and a flaky puff pastry filled with chicken and bacon in an herbaceous cream sauce. A showstopping cake cloaked in velvety buttercream and glimmering sprinkles rounds out the menu. Stemware bearing a Champagne-hued ombré finish is ideal for a bubbly Elderflower Royale made to toast the happy couple's steadfast union.

Elderflower Royale
MAKES 6 SERVINGS

6 Fabbri Amarena wild cherries in syrup
6 ounces elderflower liqueur
6 lemon zest twists
1 (750-milliliter) bottle Champagne or sparkling wine, chilled

1. In each of 6 Champagne glasses, add 1 wild cherry, 1 ounce elderflower liqueur, and 1 lemon twist. Pour Champagne to fill each glass. Serve immediately.

Elegant Pickled Shrimp
MAKES 12 APPETIZER SERVINGS

10 cups water
3 tablespoons Old Bay seasoning
2 lemons
3 pounds large fresh shrimp, peeled and deveined
¾ cup thinly sliced shallot
1 medium red bell pepper, chopped
1 teaspoon minced fresh garlic
4 fresh bay leaves
¼ cup fresh lemon juice
1 cup white wine vinegar
1 cup canola oil
1 teaspoon kosher salt
1 teaspoon crushed red pepper
1 (3.4-ounce) bottle capers, drained
1 (9.9-ounce) jar marinated baby artichoke hearts, drained and halved*
1 (14-ounce) can hearts of palm, drained and sliced*
1 (12-ounce) jar marinated mushrooms, drained
12 lemon slices
½ cup chopped fresh basil
Garnish: fresh basil leaves

1. In a large Dutch oven, bring 10 cups water and Old Bay seasoning to a boil. Slice 2 lemons and add to boiling water; let boil for 5 minutes. Add shrimp and remove from heat; let stand 15 minutes. Drain shrimp, and set aside.
2. In a large serving bowl, combine shallot and next 13 ingredients. Stir in shrimp.
3. Cover tightly, and let marinate in refrigerator overnight. Just before serving, remove bay leaves and stir in chopped basil. Garnish with basil leaves, if desired. Serve chilled with a slotted spoon.

*We used Vigo hearts of palm and marinated artichoke hearts.

Creamed Tarragon Chicken and Bacon Vol-au-Vents
MAKES 24 SERVINGS

48 ready-to-bake round puff pastry shells*
1 (16-ounce) package thick-cut bacon, cut into ½-inch pieces
1½ teaspoons kosher salt, divided
3 pounds boneless skinless chicken thighs, chopped
1½ cups finely chopped red onion
1 cup chopped celery
2 tablespoons minced garlic
¼ cup unsalted butter
4 tablespoons all-purpose flour
2 cups chicken stock
1 cup heavy whipping cream
2 tablespoons chopped fresh tarragon
2 tablespoons chopped fresh thyme
½ teaspoon ground red pepper
½ teaspoon ground black pepper
Garnish: fresh tarragon leaves, fresh thyme leaves, thinly sliced green onion

1. Bake pastry shells according to package directions until golden brown and puffed. Use the tip of a knife to remove lids; discard or reserve for another use. Remove any uncooked pastry on inside of shells by scraping with tines of a fork. Set shells aside.
2. In a heavy-duty Dutch oven, cook bacon over medium heat, stirring often, until crisp, about 10 minutes. Remove using a slotted spoon, reserving 2 tablespoons drippings in pan; let drain on paper towels.
3. Sprinkle 1 teaspoon salt on chicken.

In Dutch oven with reserved bacon drippings, cook chicken over medium heat, stirring often, until cooked through, about 8 to 10 minutes. (Chicken doesn't have to be brown.) Remove chicken from pan using a slotted spoon; set aside.
4. In same pan, cook onion, celery, and garlic over medium heat, stirring often, until onion is soft, about 10 minutes. Remove and set aside.
5. In same pan, heat butter over medium heat until melted. Add flour, whisking until mixture begins to brown, about 2 to 3 minutes. Whisk in stock and cream. Bring to a boil over high heat, whisking constantly; reduce heat to medium-low and simmer. Add cooked chicken, bacon, and onion mixture; cook until mixture begins to thicken, about 6 to 8 minutes. Stir in tarragon, thyme, red pepper, black pepper, and remaining ½ teaspoon salt.
6. For each serving, spoon about ⅓ cup chicken mixture into each of 2 pastry shells. Garnish with tarragon, thyme, and green onion, if desired.

*We used Pepperidge Farm Puff Pastry Shells.

Golden Anniversary Cake
MAKES 1 (9-INCH) CAKE

1½ cups unsalted butter, softened
2½ cups sugar
1½ cups whole milk
2 teaspoons vanilla extract
3½ cups unsifted cake flour
1 tablespoon baking powder
½ teaspoon kosher salt
7 large egg whites
Vanilla Buttercream Frosting (recipe follows)
Gold cake decorating sprinkles*

1. Preheat oven to 350°. Spray 3 (9-inch) round cake pans with baking spray with flour.
2. In the bowl of a stand mixer fitted with the paddle attachment, beat butter and sugar at medium speed until fluffy, about 2 to 3 minutes.
3. In a large bowl, stir together milk and vanilla. In another bowl, whisk together flour, baking powder, and salt. With mixer on low speed, add flour mixture to butter mixture, alternately with milk mixture, beginning and ending with flour mixture. Beat just until blended after each addition.
4. In a large bowl, beat egg whites with a mixer at medium speed until stiff peaks form; gently fold into batter. Pour batter into prepared pans.
5. Bake until a wooden pick inserted in center comes out clean, 24 to 27 minutes. Let cool in pans on wire racks for 10 minutes. Remove from pans; let cool completely on wire racks.
6. Spread Vanilla Buttercream Frosting between layers (about 1 cup per layer) and on top and sides of cake. Decorate as desired with sprinkles.

*We used Wilton.

VANILLA BUTTERCREAM FROSTING
MAKES 8 CUPS

2 cups unsalted butter, softened
½ teaspoon kosher salt
9 cups confectioners' sugar
¼ cup whole milk
1 tablespoon vanilla extract

1. In a large bowl, beat butter and salt with a mixer at medium speed until creamy, 1 to 2 minutes. With mixer at low speed, gradually add sugar, milk, and vanilla, beating until fluffy and smooth, about 2 minutes.

Perfect Parties | 123

Love Blossoms

HOST AN EASY-BREEZY BRUNCH TO REVEL IN THE SOARING SPIRITS OF A NEWLY ENGAGED TWOSOME.

Perfect Parties

126 | Perfect Parties

DISPLAY OF AFFECTION

Treat the happy couple to a fête that exudes the simple beauty of a love truly meant to be. Craft a sense of casual panache using basic dishware and airy linen fabrics in white and blue. For no-fuss flowers, mix azaleas and other garden cuttings with pretty store-bought blooms in clusters of glass bottles.

Fresh Fruit Salad
MAKES 10 TO 12 SERVINGS

6 cups honeydew spheres
   (about 1 large honeydew)
6 grapefruits, sectioned
3 naval oranges, sectioned
1 pint fresh blueberries
6 tablespoons honey
3 tablespoons chopped fresh mint

1. In a large bowl, gently stir together honeydew, grapefruit, oranges, blueberries, honey, and mint. Serve immediately, or refrigerate for up to 2 hours.

Heirloom Tomato Shrimp and Grits
MAKES 12 SERVINGS

12 cups water
3 cups grits
¾ cup unsalted butter
2½ tablespoons kosher salt, divided
1 tablespoon garlic powder
3 cups shredded Monterey Jack cheese
1 tablespoon olive oil
1½ cups diced red onion
1½ pounds large fresh shrimp, peeled
   and deveined (tails left on)
3 cloves garlic, minced
¾ cup fresh lemon juice
½ cup chopped fresh parsley
1 pint heirloom cherry tomatoes, halved
Garnish: fresh baby arugula, crumbled
   feta cheese

1. In a medium saucepan, bring 12 cups water to a boil over medium-high heat. Slowly whisk in grits, butter, 1½ tablespoons kosher salt, and garlic powder. Reduce heat to medium-low; cook, stirring occasionally, until thickened, about 20 minutes. Stir in Monterey Jack cheese until smooth.
2. In a large skillet, heat oil over medium-high heat. Add onion to pan; cook until tender, about 3 minutes. Add shrimp, garlic, lemon juice, and remaining 1 tablespoon salt; cook until shrimp are pink and firm, about 5 minutes. Stir in parsley and tomatoes. Serve shrimp over grits. Garnish with arugula and feta, if desired.

Lavender French 75
MAKES 12 SERVINGS

2½ cups Lavender Simple Syrup
   (see Iced Tea Bar instructions)
1½ cups dry gin
¼ cup fresh lemon juice
2 (750-milliliter) bottles brut sparkling
   wine
Garnish: lavender blossom

1. In a large pitcher, stir together Lavender Simple Syrup, gin, and lemon juice. Pour ⅓ cup gin mixture into a Champagne flute, and top with ½ cup sparkling wine. Repeat with remaining gin mixture and sparkling wine. Garnish with lavender blossom, if desired.

Perfect Parties | 129

Iced Tea Bar

For a fun beverage option, set up a station with unsweetened tea and a selection of sweet syrups.

CLASSIC SIMPLE SYRUP
MAKES 2 CUPS

2 cups water
2 cups sugar

1. In a small saucepan, bring water and sugar to a simmer, stirring occasionally. Remove from heat. Refrigerate until completely cool. Syrup will keep in an airtight container for up to 1 month.

RASPBERRY SIMPLE SYRUP
MAKES 2 CUPS

2 cups water
2 cups sugar
2 (6-ounce) containers raspberries

1. In a small saucepan, bring water and sugar to a simmer, stirring occasionally. Remove from heat, and add raspberries, crushing slightly. Steep in liquid for 20 minutes.
2. Strain mixture through a fine-mesh sieve, discarding raspberry pulp. Refrigerate until completely cool. Syrup will keep in an airtight container for up to 1 month.

LAVENDER SIMPLE SYRUP
MAKES 4 CUPS

4 cups water
2½ cups sugar
1 cup lavender blossoms
¼ cup blueberries

1. In a medium saucepan, bring water and sugar to a simmer, stirring occasionally. Remove from heat, and add lavender and blueberries; steep in liquid for 20 minutes.
2. Strain through a fine-mesh sieve, discarding lavender and blueberries. Refrigerate until completely cool. Syrup will keep in an airtight container for up to 1 month.

Blissful Beginnings

WITH A SPREAD OF SAVORY EATS AND DELECTABLE BITES, CELEBRATE NEWLYWEDS AT A GRACIOUS HOUSEWARMING PARTY.

HEARTFELT WELCOME

Extend well wishes to a just-married couple settling into their first abode at a get-together complete with gifts and goodies that symbolize prosperity, such as bread, honey, and houseplants. An eclectic blend of mismatched china, antique vessels, rustic wooden trays, and modish table linens keeps the décor fuss free. Lively floral arrangements and potted plants make the house feel like home; bouquets of roses, hydrangeas, peonies, ranunculus, scabiosas, and greenery dance about the room at varying heights for a dynamic showcase that echoes gardens in bloom just outside the window. An artful cheese board and finger foods satiate guests' appetites while they catch up with one another. Tantalizing fare includes mini turkey burgers, a creamy green-onion-and-bacon dip, and Prosciutto and Fig Flatbread drizzled with a balsamic glaze. Before bidding farewell, indulge in white chocolate–strawberry fudge and toast the happy homeowners.

Bacon and Green Onion Dip
MAKES ABOUT 2 CUPS

1 (8-ounce) package cream cheese, room temperature
1 cup grated Parmesan cheese
½ cup mayonnaise, room temperature
¼ cup sour cream, room temperature
1 cup cooked, crumbled bacon, divided
1 cup sliced green onion, divided
⅛ teaspoon garlic powder
⅛ teaspoon onion powder
Homemade Potato Chips (recipe follows)

1. In a medium bowl, whisk together cream cheese, Parmesan, mayonnaise, sour cream, ¾ cup bacon, ¾ cup green onion, garlic powder, and onion powder. Sprinkle with remaining ¼ cup bacon and remaining ¼ cup green onion. Serve with Homemade Potato Chips.

HOMEMADE POTATO CHIPS
MAKES ABOUT 12 CUPS

4 large russet potatoes, sliced ⅛ inch thick
¾ cup white distilled vinegar
Canola oil, for frying
1 teaspoon kosher salt
1 teaspoon paprika

1. Rinse and drain potatoes.
2. In a large bowl, add potatoes, vinegar, and water to cover. Let stand for 30 minutes to 1 hour. Drain and dry.
3. In a Dutch oven, add 2 inches of oil and heat over medium heat until a candy thermometer registers 300°. Working in small batches, add potatoes and cook, stirring constantly, until golden brown, 10 to 15 minutes.
4. Using a slotted spoon, remove chips from oil. Let drain on paper towels. Toss with salt and paprika.

Prosciutto and Fig Flatbread
MAKES 4 FLATBREAD PIZZAS

2 (14.1-ounce) packages flatbread*
1 (13-ounce) jar fig jam
1 (8-ounce) package fresh mozzarella pearls
4 (3-ounce) packages sliced prosciutto
1 (4-ounce) package goat cheese
1 (4-ounce) bag fresh baby arugula
1 (2-ounce) jar pine nuts, toasted
Balsamic glaze*

1. Preheat oven to 425°.
2. Top each flatbread with fig jam, mozzarella pearls, prosciutto, and goat cheese.
3. Bake until flatbread is golden brown and cheese is melted, 15 to 20 minutes.
4. Top cooked flatbread with arugula and pine nuts. Drizzle with balsamic glaze.

*We used Stonefire Artisan Flatbread and Bertolli Balsamic Glaze.

Turkey Sliders with Red Onion Jam
MAKES 12

2 pounds ground turkey
1 tablespoon plus ¼ teaspoon kosher salt, divided
1 teaspoon ground black pepper
½ cup mayonnaise
1 teaspoon lemon zest
2 tablespoons fresh lemon juice
2 cloves garlic, finely chopped
½ teaspoon Dijon mustard
2 tablespoons vegetable oil
1 (12-pack) slider buns, toasted
Red Onion Jam (recipe follows)
Red leaf lettuce

1. Form ground turkey into 12 (2½-ounce) patties. Sprinkle each side evenly with 1 tablespoon salt and pepper.
2. In a small bowl, combine mayonnaise, lemon zest and juice, garlic, mustard, and remaining ¼ teaspoon salt. Cover and refrigerate until ready to cook.

Perfect Parties | 137

3. In a large skillet, heat oil over medium heat. Cook turkey patties until nicely seared on both sides and an instant-read thermometer inserted into the center registers 165°, 15 to 20 minutes. Let rest 5 minutes before assembling.
4. Serve on slider buns with mayonnaise mixture, Red Onion Jam, and lettuce.

RED ONION JAM
MAKES ABOUT 1 CUP

1 tablespoon vegetable oil
4 cups diced red onion
1 tablespoon sugar
¼ cup red wine vinegar
1 tablespoon Dijon mustard
1 teaspoon kosher salt
½ teaspoon ground black pepper

1. In a small saucepan, heat oil over medium heat. Add onion and stir to coat; cook until onions are tender, stirring constantly, about 10 minutes. Add sugar, vinegar, mustard, salt, and pepper; cook until liquid has evaporated, 5 to 7 minutes. Let cool completely. Cover and refrigerate until ready to use.

Strawberry Swirl Fudge
MAKES ABOUT 36 PIECES

2 cups sugar
1 cup heavy whipping cream
½ cup unsalted butter
1 teaspoon kosher salt
6 (4-ounce) bars white chocolate, chopped
2 (7-ounce) jars marshmallow fluff
2 teaspoons vanilla extract
1 (1.2-ounce) bag freeze-dried strawberries, crushed and divided
2 teaspoons strawberry extract
10 drops red liquid food coloring*

1. Line an 8x8-inch baking pan with parchment paper, letting paper extend over edges of pan by 2 inches. Spray parchment paper with baking spray.
2. In a medium saucepan, bring sugar, cream, butter, and salt to a boil over medium heat, stirring constantly, until a candy thermometer registers 234°. Remove from heat and stir in white chocolate, marshmallow fluff, and vanilla, stirring vigorously, until combined.
3. Add half of white chocolate fudge into prepared pan. To remaining half, add ¼ cup freeze-dried strawberries, strawberry extract, and food coloring; stir until well combined. Drop dollops of strawberry fudge on top of white chocolate fudge; swirl with a knife. Sprinkle remaining freeze-dried strawberries on top.
4. Refrigerate for at least 4 hours. Cut into 1-inch squares. Store in an airtight container for up to 5 days.

*We used Wilton Color Right red food coloring.

Perfect Parties | 139

Curated Delight

Swap a grazing board for a personal plate of mini morsels arranged at each place setting—a creative twist on the traditional charcuterie tray.

1. Select a small dish from your china collection that coordinates with your place settings. Depending on how many dishes you will use in your setting, a salad or bread plate will work perfectly. Alternatively, use miniature wooden cutting boards for homespun flair.

2. Arrange a selection of cheeses, crackers, nuts, salumi, and fresh or dried fruit on the dish. Choose a variety of bites both sweet and savory that will complement each other, as a mix of flavors makes for the most satisfying charcuterie spread.

3. Once you are happy with the individual arrangements, assemble your place cards. We used a 2-inch-wide circle punch to cut out paper disks. You can choose to make all your place cards from one sheet of paper, or you can mix and match different colors and prints for an eclectic feel.

4. Employing your best penmanship, accent the cut paper disks with each guest's name. A metallic marker adds an elevated touch to the inscription.

5. Use double-sided tape to sandwich a short wood or metal skewer between the inscribed card and a blank disk.

6. Nestle the place card into a sturdy slice of fruit or a small piece of cheese for a pleasing display that's as tasty as it is charming.

Happily Ever After

FAIRY TALES REALLY DO COME TRUE! DOTE ON A BRIDE-TO-BE WITH A SLEEPING BEAUTY–INSPIRED BRIDAL SHOWER.

Perfect Parties | 143

ENCHANTED APPEAL

Fashion a tablescape of succulents, ferns, and flowers galore to echo the idyllic surrounds of the woodland cottage where young Princess Aurora lived with her fairy guardians. A bed of moss forms the base for a floral centerpiece, filled out with swags of greenery. To showcase a scrumptious multilayered cake, stack a wood-slice tower as a tribute to Sleeping Beauty's castle quarters.

SWEET DREAMS

The menu for this fairy-tale fête features mini confections both delicate and delicious. Scalloped-edge sugar cookies, iced in pretty pastel hues, sparkle alongside pistachio-sprinkled truffles, grown-up gummy squares, and decadent almond roca—especially when displayed on glass serving pieces. As a nod to Charles Perrault's original story, cut a square from a vintage book and then nestle a collection of succulents amid the prose.

Perfect Parties | 147

Chocolate-Brandy Truffles
MAKES ABOUT 32

12 (1-ounce) squares semisweet chocolate, chopped
⅓ cup heavy cream
1 tablespoon brandy
1 teaspoon vanilla extract
1 (16-ounce) package chocolate-flavored candy coating
Garnish: crushed pistachios

1. In a double boiler, combine chocolate, cream, brandy, and vanilla extract. Stir until melted and smooth. Cover, and place in refrigerator until firm enough to roll into balls, about 2 hours.
2. Line a baking sheet with parchment paper. Using a small 1-inch spring-loaded ice cream scoop, scoop mixture into portions. Using your hands, roll each portion into a ball. Place back in refrigerator until firm, about 1 hour.
3. Place candy coating in a microwave-safe bowl. Microwave on high in 30-second intervals until melted and smooth (about 1½ minutes total). Dredge balls in candy coating to coat. Set on parchment paper to dry. Garnish immediately with crushed pistachios, if desired.

Lemon Sugar Cookies
MAKES ABOUT 24

1 cup granulated sugar
2 tablespoons fresh lemon zest
1 cup unsalted butter, softened
½ cup confectioners' sugar
2 large eggs
2 teaspoons vanilla extract
1 teaspoon coconut extract
3 cups all-purpose flour
1 teaspoon ground ginger
½ teaspoon kosher salt
¼ teaspoon baking powder
Meringue Powder Icing (recipe follows)
Garnish: sparkling gold sugar, gold dragées

1. In a small bowl, combine granulated sugar and lemon zest, rubbing with your fingers. Allow to sit for 15 minutes.
2. In the bowl of a stand mixer fitted with the paddle attachment, beat butter, sugar mixture, and confectioners' sugar at medium-high speed until creamy. Add eggs, one at a time, beating well after each addition.
3. Add extracts, beating to combine.
4. In a separate medium bowl, sift together flour, ginger, salt, and baking powder. Reduce mixer speed to low. Add flour mixture to butter mixture, beating to combine.
5. Roll dough between two pieces of parchment paper to a ¼-inch thickness. Place in freezer until firm, 15 to 20 minutes.
6. Preheat oven to 350°. Line 2 rimmed baking sheets with parchment paper; set aside.
7. Using a 3-inch fluted round cookie cutter, cut as many cookies as possible. Repeat with remaining dough. Place cookies on prepared baking sheets. Bake until edges are lightly browned, 10 minutes. Let cool on baking sheets for 5 minutes; remove to wire racks to let cool completely. Paint with Meringue Powder Icing. Garnish with sparkling sugar and gold dragées, if desired.

MERINGUE POWDER ICING
MAKES ABOUT 2½ CUPS

¼ cup cold water
3 tablespoons meringue powder
2 cups confectioners' sugar
Assorted food colorings

1. In the bowl of a stand mixer fitted with the whisk attachment, beat water and meringue powder until frothy. Whisk in confectioners' sugar until smooth. Divide into bowls, and whisk in desired food colorings. Use immediately. Paint cookies using small pastry brushes.

Almond Roca
MAKES 2 POUNDS

1½ cups sliced almonds, toasted, divided
2 cups firmly packed light brown sugar
2 cups unsalted butter
2 (12-ounce) packages milk chocolate chips
1 tablespoon vegetable shortening
Garnish: edible gold leaf, gold sparkling sugar

1. Sprinkle ¾ cup almonds onto the bottom of a jelly roll pan; set aside.
2. In a medium saucepan, combine sugar and butter over medium-high heat. Cook, stirring frequently, until mixture registers 290°. (Watch carefully after mixture reaches 280° to prevent it from burning.) Remove from heat. Pour evenly over sliced almonds. Let cool slightly.
3. Meanwhile, in a medium bowl, microwave chocolate chips and shortening on high in 30-second intervals, stirring between each, until completely melted and smooth, about 1½ minutes total. Pour chocolate over almond layer. Sprinkle with remaining ¾ cup almonds. Garnish with gold leaf and sparkling sugar, if desired. Allow mixture to set, about 2 hours.
4. Once mixture is set, break into pieces, using a knife. Store covered at room temperature for up to 5 days.

Pink Grapefruit Jellies
MAKES ABOUT 65

1⅓ cups pink grapefruit juice, divided
2 tablespoons Campari
4 (0.25-ounce) envelopes unflavored gelatin or 1 (1-ounce) box
2½ cups superfine or caster sugar, divided
1 (18-ounce) jar plum jelly
1 teaspoon clear vanilla extract
Garnish: edible gold leaf

1. In a small bowl, whisk together ⅔ cup grapefruit juice, Campari, and gelatin. Let sit for 5 minutes.
2. Meanwhile, in a medium saucepan, combine remaining ⅔ cup grapefruit juice and 1½ cups sugar. Bring to a boil over medium-high heat. Cook, stirring constantly, until sugar dissolves, about 5 minutes. Add jelly and vanilla, and whisk to combine. Return to boil, and cook until thick, about 2 minutes.
3. Add gelatin mixture to jelly mixture, whisking to combine. Strain mixture into an 8x11-inch baking pan. Chill for 4 hours or overnight. Cut into squares.
4. In a small bowl, place remaining 1 cup sugar. Toss jellies in sugar to coat. Garnish with edible gold leaf, if desired. Store covered in refrigerator for up to 1 week.

Lavender Pink Lemonade Punch
MAKES 2½ QUARTS

1 (12-ounce) can frozen pink lemonade concentrate, thawed
Lavender Simple Syrup (recipe follows)
½ cup Campari
1 liter club soda, chilled
1 (750-milliliter) bottle Champagne, chilled
Garnish: lemon slices

1. In a large pitcher, whisk together lemonade, simple syrup, Campari, and club soda. Add Champagne. Garnish with lemon, if desired. Serve immediately.

LAVENDER SIMPLE SYRUP
MAKES 1 CUP

1 cup water
2 cups sugar
1 tablespoon fresh lavender blossoms

1. In a small saucepan, combine water and sugar. Bring mixture to a boil over high heat. Reduce heat to medium, and simmer for 10 minutes. Remove from heat; add lavender, and let cool completely. Chill for at least 2 hours. Strain mixture, discarding solids, and store covered in the refrigerator for up to 3 weeks.

Rosette to Impress

Follow this step-by-step tutorial to fold a napkin into a dainty flower-shaped accent for any tablescape.

1. Fold a square linen in half to create a large triangle. Roll the long edge or base of the triangle toward the point, leaving a small triangle of fabric flat on the table.

2. Beginning on one end, tightly roll up the long edge to within about 4 inches of the opposite end.

3. A flat base allows you to stand up the napkin. Continue wrapping the tail around and then tuck it in near the base.

4. Separate the top points to fold down each piece of fabric.

5. Flip over the design and adjust the pieces to resemble leaves. We added a pair of freshly clipped leaves for a final flourish.

4

Celebrations of Childhood

HONOR LIFE'S MOST PRECIOUS GIFTS, WHETHER SHOWERING MOMS-TO-BE OR TREATING KIDS AND TEENS TO FUN-FILLED AFFAIRS.

Bundle of Joy

SHOWER AN EXPECTANT MOTHER WITH BABY BOOKS AND GOODIES, PLAYING UP A ROSY PALETTE THAT'S MOST APROPOS.

Perfect Parties | 155

TRUE TREASURES

A spectrum of pinks, interspersed with dashes of peach and white, remind those gathered of the blessing soon to arrive. Greet guests with a lush floral wreath studded with pink hypericum berries and finished with a satin bow. Silver rattles and a personalized cup reflect time-honored traditions and coordinate with passed-down sterling vases. Tuck in a few blooms, borrowed from overflowing arrangements on the table and sideboard, to bring the thematic color scheme full circle. Both beautiful and sentimental, children's books kindle reminiscences of bedtimes gone by and mark the beginning of a new chapter for the family. Tiered stands and a mix of platters present savory morsels and bite-size desserts—from biscuits topped with smoked salmon rosettes to fruit-filled petits fours capped with dainty edible flowers.

Perfect Parties

Biscuit Crostini with Smoked Salmon Rosettes
MAKES 24

1 (8-ounce) package sliced smoked salmon
1 (8-ounce) package cream cheese, softened
1 tablespoon loosely packed chopped fresh dill
½ teaspoon ground black pepper
1 clove garlic, finely minced
Seasoned Biscuits (recipe follows)
Garnish: small fresh basil leaves

1. In the work bowl of a food processor, place salmon, cream cheese, dill, pepper, and garlic; pulse until smooth. Transfer to a small bowl, and cover with plastic wrap. Refrigerate for at least 1 hour.
2. Using a Wilton 1M star tip, pipe mousse onto Seasoned Biscuits in a spiral motion starting in center to create a rosette shape. The smoked salmon mousse can be made up to a day ahead and refrigerated, but should be served immediately once piped on the biscuits. Garnish with basil, if desired.

SEASONED BISCUITS
MAKES 24

1 teaspoon poppy seeds
1 teaspoon sesame seeds
1 teaspoon dried garlic
1 teaspoon dried onion
½ teaspoon kosher salt
1 (24-ounce) bag frozen tea biscuits*, thawed
¼ cup unsalted butter, melted

1. Preheat oven to 375°.
2. In a small bowl, combine poppy seeds, sesame seeds, dried garlic, dried onion, and salt.
3. Pat each biscuit out slightly into an oval shape. Brush with melted butter, and sprinkle with seasoning.
4. Bake for 10 minutes. Let cool for at least 10 minutes.

*We used Mary B's Tea Biscuits.

Baby Carrots with Fresh Herb Dip
MAKES ABOUT 6 SERVINGS

1 (8-ounce) package cream cheese, softened
1 cup sour cream
4 to 5 green onions, chopped (white and green parts)
¼ cup chopped fresh parsley
2 tablespoons chopped fresh dill
1 teaspoon kosher salt
½ teaspoon ground black pepper
35 to 40 petite rainbow carrots

1. In the work bowl of a food processor, place cream cheese, sour cream, green onion, parsley, dill, salt, and pepper; process until smooth. Refrigerate until ready to serve.
2. Spoon about ¼ cup dip into each individual serving cup; place 5 to 6 carrots in each cup. Serve immediately. Dip will keep refrigerated for up to 2 weeks.

Lemon-Blackberry Petits Fours
MAKES ABOUT 20

Cake:
1½ cups unsalted butter, softened
3 cups granulated sugar
6 large eggs, room temperature
3 cups all-purpose flour
½ teaspoon kosher salt
⅛ teaspoon baking soda
1 (8-ounce) container sour cream, room temperature
¼ cup to ½ cup blackberry preserves
Lemon Buttercream (recipe follows)

Glaze:
6 cups confectioners' sugar, sifted
½ cup water
2 tablespoons light corn syrup
1 teaspoon almond extract
1 teaspoon vanilla extract
¾ cup white chocolate chips
Garnish: edible flowers

1. Preheat oven to 325°. Line 2 (13x9-inch) metal baking pans with parchment paper.
2. For cake: In the bowl of a stand mixer fitted with the paddle attachment, beat butter and sugar at medium speed until fluffy, 3 to 4 minutes, stopping to scrape sides of bowl. Add eggs, one at a time, beating well after each addition.
3. In a medium bowl, whisk together flour, salt, and baking soda. With mixer on low speed, gradually add flour mixture to butter mixture alternately with sour cream, beginning and ending with flour mixture, beating just until combined after each addition. Divide batter between prepared pans (smoothing tops if necessary).
4. Bake until a wooden pick inserted in center comes out clean, 25 to 30 minutes. Let cool in pans for 10 minutes. Remove from pans, and let cool completely on wire racks.
5. Using a long serrated knife, trim top of cake layers. Spread blackberry

Perfect Parties | 161

a crust from forming. Let petits fours set until dry, about 1 hour. Remove petits fours using a small offset spatula, and place on a serving tray. Garnish with edible flowers, if desired.

LEMON BUTTERCREAM
MAKES ABOUT 2 CUPS

⅓ cup salted butter, softened
2¼ cups sifted confectioners' sugar
½ teaspoon vanilla extract
1½ tablespoons fresh lemon juice
1 tablespoon whole milk

1. In a medium bowl, beat butter with a mixer at medium speed until creamy. Gradually add confectioners' sugar and vanilla, beating until well combined. Add lemon juice and milk, and beat at high speed until smooth and spreadable.

White Chocolate-Covered Strawberries
MAKES ABOUT 24

1 (10-ounce) bag white chocolate melting wafers*
2 (16-ounce) containers fresh strawberries, room temperature

1. In a small microwave-safe bowl, microwave chocolate on medium in 30-second intervals, stirring between each, until chocolate is melted and smooth (about 1½ minutes total). Dip one strawberry at a time in melted white chocolate, and place on a sheet of parchment paper. Place any remaining melted white chocolate in a piping bag, and drizzle over strawberries. Let chocolate set. Refrigerate for up to 1 day.

*We used Ghirardelli.

preserves onto one cake layer. Top with second cake layer, cut side down. Spread Lemon Buttercream onto top of cake. Place cake in freezer, and top with a sheet of parchment paper, rubbing gently with palm to smooth buttercream. Freeze for 2 hours.
6. Remove parchment, and trim edges of cake using a serrated knife. Cut cake into 1-inch squares.
7. For glaze: In a large microwave-safe bowl, whisk together confectioners' sugar, ½ cup water, corn syrup, and extracts. Microwave on high in 30-second intervals, stirring between each, until smooth (about 1 minute total). Add chocolate chips, and stir until melted. Microwave in 10-second intervals until chocolate is fully melted.
8. Cover work surface with a piece of plastic wrap. Place a wire rack on top of four cans set over plastic wrap. Using a short wooden skewer, prick each petit four in center about halfway through. Dip in warm glaze, letting excess drip off. Thread skewer through wire rack, bringing petit four to rest on wire rack. (This will allow any excess glaze to drip off and create clean bottom edges once dry.) Reheat glaze while working to keep

Perfect Parties | 163

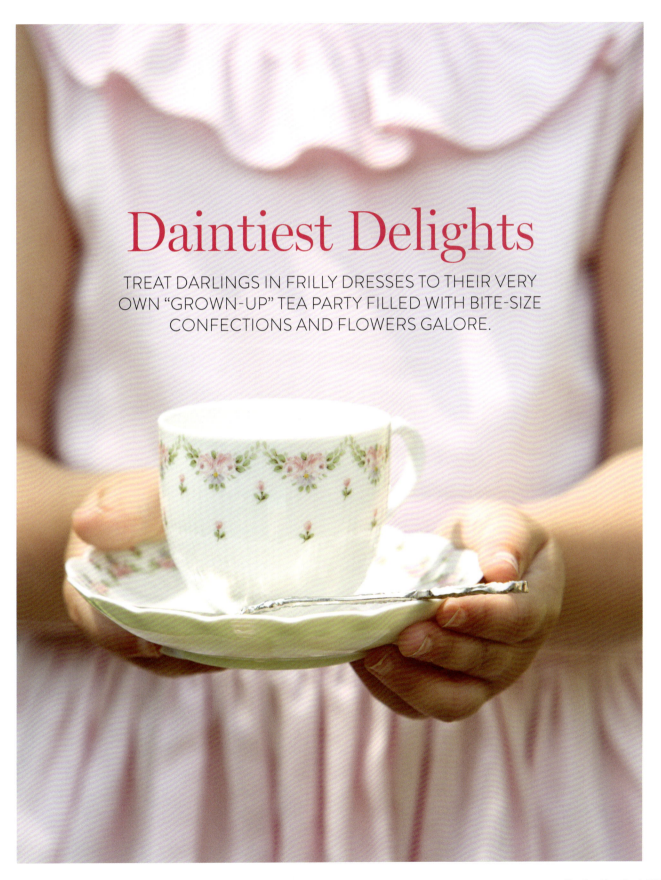

Daintiest Delights

TREAT DARLINGS IN FRILLY DRESSES TO THEIR VERY OWN "GROWN-UP" TEA PARTY FILLED WITH BITE-SIZE CONFECTIONS AND FLOWERS GALORE.

TICKLED PINK

Dressed in pristine whites and soft pinks, a fanciful child-size table welcomes the littlest ladies for an afternoon to remember. Tea sets dotted with the most delicate of buds and blossoms are certain to elicit enthusiastic giggles and squeals. Further the enchantment with traditional but kid-friendly morsels, such as dressed-up tea sandwiches and heart-shaped scones—a sweet assortment for an even sweeter day.

3. To assemble sandwiches, pipe peanut butter mixture along the edges of whole bread flowers; fill in the rest of the flower shape. Spread a small amount of strawberry jam on top of peanut butter mixture. Top with bread flowers with cutouts. Fill cutouts with a small amount of jam. Serve immediately, or drape with damp paper towels to prevent sandwiches from drying out.

> **KITCHEN TIP:**
> Freeze bread before cutting flower shapes for crisp, clean outlines. Place bread flowers in a resealable plastic bag to thaw and prevent drying out.

Vanilla Mini Cupcakes with Vanilla Buttercream
MAKES 48

½ cup unsalted butter, softened
¾ cup extra-fine sugar
2 large eggs
1½ cups cake flour*
1½ teaspoons baking powder
¼ teaspoon kosher salt
¼ cup whole milk
¼ cup sour cream
1½ teaspoons vanilla extract
Vanilla Buttercream (recipe follows)
Garnish: pearlescent sugar*

1. Preheat oven to 350°. Line 48 mini muffin cups with paper liners.
2. In a large bowl, beat butter and extra-fine sugar with a mixer at high speed until light and fluffy, 3 to 5 minutes. Add eggs, one at a time, beating well after each addition.
3. In a medium bowl, whisk together flour, baking powder, and salt. In a small bowl, whisk together milk, sour cream, and vanilla. Gradually add flour mixture to butter mixture alternately with milk mixture, beginning and ending with flour mixture, beating just until combined after each addition. Using a 2-teaspoon scoop, drop batter into prepared muffin cups.
4. Bake until very lightly browned and a wooden pick inserted in center come out clean, about 10 minutes. Let cool

Pink Heart Scones
MAKES 11

2 cups all-purpose flour
⅓ cup granulated sugar
2 teaspoons baking powder
½ teaspoon salt
¼ cup cold unsalted butter, softened
¾ cup plus 1 tablespoon heavy whipping cream, chilled
½ teaspoon vanilla extract
¼ teaspoon almond extract
⅛ teaspoon liquid red food coloring
Garnish: confectioners' sugar

1. Preheat oven to 350°. Line a rimmed baking sheet with parchment paper.
2. In a large bowl, whisk together flour, granulated sugar, baking powder, and salt. Using a pastry blender, cut in butter until mixture is crumbly.
3. In a small bowl, stir together cream, extracts, and food coloring. Add cream mixture to flour mixture, stirring just until mixture comes together. (If dough seems dry, add more cream, 1 tablespoon at a time, until dough is uniformly moist.)
4. Working gently, bring mixture together with hands until a dough forms. Turn out dough onto a lightly floured surface, and knead gently 3 to 5 times. Roll dough to ½-inch thickness. Using a 2¾-inch heart-shaped cutter, cut dough, rerolling scraps as necessary. Place scones 2 inches apart on prepared pan.
5. Bake until edges are golden brown and a wooden pick inserted in center comes out clean, 18 to 20 minutes. Garnish with confectioners' sugar, if desired.

Peanut Butter and Jam Flower Sandwiches
MAKES 12

4 ounces cream cheese, softened
½ cup creamy peanut butter
12 large slices white sandwich bread
⅓ cup seedless strawberry jam

1. In a medium bowl, beat cream cheese and peanut butter with a mixer at medium-high speed until creamy. Place mixture in a piping bag fitted with a medium open tip (Wilton #12).
2. Using a 2¼-inch flower-shaped cutter, cut 24 flower shapes from bread slices. Using a 1-inch round cutter, cut holes from center of 12 flowers.

completely. Place Vanilla Buttercream in a piping bag fitted with a large open-star tip (Wilton #1M), and pipe a rosette on top of each cupcake. Garnish with pearlescent sugar, if desired. Refrigerate in a covered container until serving time.

*We used Swans Down Cake Flour and India Tree Sparkling Sugar Confetti.

VANILLA BUTTERCREAM
MAKES 3 CUPS

5 cups confectioners' sugar
1 cup unsalted butter, softened
2 tablespoons whole milk
1 tablespoon vanilla extract
¼ teaspoon kosher salt

1. In a large bowl, beat confectioners' sugar, butter, milk, vanilla, and salt with a mixer at high speed until combined. Use immediately.

MAKE-AHEAD TIP: Buttercream can be made a day in advance and refrigerated in a covered container. Let it come to room temperature, and beat with a mixer for 1 minute before piping.

Pink Cotton Candy Macarons
MAKES 50 SANDWICH COOKIES

2½ cups confectioners' sugar
2½ cups almond flour
6 large egg whites, room temperature and divided
Pink food coloring* (optional)
1 cup granulated sugar
¼ cup water
⅛ teaspoon egg white powder
1 teaspoon raspberry extract
White Chocolate Ganache (recipe follows)

1. In the work bowl of a food processor, combine confectioners' sugar and almond flour; process until finely ground. In a large bowl, beat 3 egg whites and almond flour mixture with a mixer at medium speed until combined. Add desired amount of food coloring to tint almond mixture, if desired.

2. In a small saucepan, heat granulated sugar and ¼ cup water over medium heat. Cook until mixture reaches soft-ball stage (234° to 240° on a candy thermometer).
3. In the bowl of a stand mixer fitted with the whisk attachment, beat egg white powder and remaining 3 egg whites at high speed until soft peaks form. Slowly add hot syrup to egg whites, beating at medium speed until meringue has thickened and cooled, about 3 minutes. (Bowl should be slightly warm to the touch.) Beat in raspberry extract. Fold meringue into almond mixture with a spatula, a little at a time, until combined and batter is loose. (Batter should fall in thick ribbons from the spatula.)
4. Preheat oven to 270°. Line several rimmed baking sheets with silicone baking mats or parchment paper.
5. Place batter in piping bag fitted with a medium round tip (Wilton #12). Pipe batter onto prepared pans in quarter-size rounds. Drop pans onto countertops several times to release air bubbles. Let stand for 20 minutes to create a skin on macarons. (Finger should not stick to surface of macaron.)
6. Bake until firm to the touch, 17 to 20 minutes. (Place finger on macaron and try to wiggle macaron. If macaron wiggles, continue to bake until macaron is firm.) Let cool completely on pans. Wrap macarons in groups of 6 in plastic wrap, and place in an airtight container. Refrigerate overnight before filling.
7. Place White Chocolate Ganache in a pastry bag fitted with a medium round tip (Wilton #12). Pipe filling onto flat side of half of macarons. Place remaining macarons, flat side down, on top of filling. Keep refrigerated until serving time.

*We used Wilton.

WHITE CHOCOLATE GANACHE
MAKES 1¼ CUPS

¾ cup heavy whipping cream
2 cups white chocolate chips

1. In a medium saucepan, heat cream over medium high heat until simmering but not boiling. Remove from heat; add white chocolate chips, whisking until chocolate is melted and mixture is completely smooth. Pour mixture into a covered container, and refrigerate overnight.

Oh Happy Day

A SPECIAL BIRTHDAY IS MADE EVEN BRIGHTER WITH RIBBONS AND BOWS INSPIRED BY MERRY MAYPOLES.

ALL THE FRILLS

This magical party in the park proves that wishes really do come true. A pretty palette of pink, blue, and green sets the stage for a parade of friendly wildlife creatures marching across the playful china. Pillows in coordinating colors surround the table to provide cozy seating for little partygoers when it's time for a quick break from fun and games. Tiny treat bags adorned with roses are take-home goodies guests will relish as much as the day's menu: creamy strawberry smoothies, crispy chicken tenders, rainbow-inspired fruit cups, and scrumptious cupcakes topped with sparkling flower-shaped candies.

Perfect Parties | 175

Rainbow Fruit Cups with Vanilla Honey
MAKES ABOUT 12 SERVINGS

¼ cup honey
½ tablespoon vanilla bean paste
1 (1-pound) container fresh strawberries, hulled and quartered
6 clementines, peeled and sectioned
1 pineapple, cored, sliced into 6 rings, and each ring cut into 8 pieces
½ pound green grapes, halved
2 (1-pint) containers fresh blueberries
½ pound purple or red grapes, halved

1. In a large bowl, combine honey and vanilla bean paste.
2. Toss strawberries in honey mixture, and layer in bottom of serving glasses. Repeat with all remaining fruit, tossing in honey mixture and layering in glasses as desired.

Baked Pretzel Chicken Tenders
MAKES ABOUT 8 SERVINGS

4 cups pretzels, crushed
2 large eggs
1 tablespoon milk
½ cup all-purpose flour
½ teaspoon chili powder
½ teaspoon garlic powder
½ teaspoon onion powder
½ teaspoon kosher salt
½ teaspoon ground black pepper
2 (2-pound) packages chicken tenders
Buttermilk Ranch Dip (recipe follows)

1. Preheat oven to 400°. Line baking sheets with foil and spray with cooking spray.
2. Place pretzels in a large bowl. In a medium bowl, whisk together eggs and milk. In another medium bowl, whisk together flour, chili powder, garlic powder, onion powder, salt, and pepper.
3. Dredge chicken in flour mixture, shaking off excess. Dip in egg mixture, letting excess drip off. Dredge in pretzels, pressing gently to adhere. Place in a single layer on prepared pan.
4. Bake until a meat thermometer inserted in center registers 160°, 15 to 20 minutes. Serve with Buttermilk Ranch Dip.

BUTTERMILK RANCH DIP
MAKES 2 CUPS

1¾ cups low-fat buttermilk
½ cup light mayonnaise
½ (7-ounce) container light Greek yogurt
1 (1-ounce) package ranch dressing mix

1. In a small bowl, whisk together all ingredients. Refrigerate until ready to serve.

NOTE: Buttermilk Ranch Dip is best if made 24 hours in advance.

Perfect Parties | 177

Strawberry Cheesecake Smoothies
MAKES 12 SERVINGS

1 (1-pound) container fresh strawberries, hulled
1 (8-ounce) package cream cheese, softened
¼ cup honey
4 (7-ounce) containers strawberry cheesecake yogurt
1½ cups milk
Garnish: fresh strawberries

1. In the container of a blender, place strawberries; pulse until smooth. Remove from blender, and set aside.
2. Place cream cheese and honey in blender; blend until smooth. Add puréed strawberries, yogurt, and milk; blend until smooth and creamy. Freeze for 1 hour. Garnish with strawberries, if desired.

Birthday Flower Cupcakes
MAKES 24

1 (15.25-ounce) box yellow cake mix
1 cup water
½ cup vegetable oil
3 large eggs
1 cup unsalted butter, softened
¼ cup all-vegetable shortening
5 cups confectioners' sugar
1 (7-ounce) container marshmallow crème
1 tablespoon milk
Pink liquid food coloring
Edible luster dust*
48 sugar flowers*

1. Preheat oven to 350°. Line 2 (12-cup) muffin pans with paper liners.
2. In a large bowl, beat cake mix, 1 cup water, oil, and eggs with a mixer at medium speed until combined, about 2 minutes. Spoon batter into prepared muffin cups.
3. Bake until a wooden pick inserted in center comes out clean, about 20 minutes. Let cool in pans for 5 minutes. Remove from pans, and let cool completely on wire racks.
4. In the bowl of a stand mixer fitted with the paddle attachment, beat butter and shortening at medium speed until creamy. Add confectioners' sugar, marshmallow crème, and milk, beating until well combined. Add food coloring, beating until desired color is reached.
5. Place icing in a piping bag fitted with a star tip, and swirl icing onto cooled cupcakes. Brush luster dust onto sugar flowers and place on cupcakes.

We used Sunny Side Up Bakery luster dust and Wilton flowers.

Cordial Confections

Make seating your guests an extra treat with our steps for icing personalized sugar cookies that double as place markers and party favors.

1. Start with your favorite sugar cookie recipe and a shapely cookie cutter, or purchase cookies from your local bakery.

2. Make meringue powder icing. In a medium bowl, beat ¼ cup water and 3 tablespoons meringue powder with a wire whisk until frothy. Whisk in 2 cups confectioners' sugar until smooth. (Makes 2½ cups.)

3. Separate the icing into small bowls. Add food coloring to achieve your desired colors and then paint the cookies using small pastry brushes. Using a squeeze bottle or pastry bag, pipe outlines, names, and details. Sprinkle with sanding sugar.

Baskets & Bounty

RELISH A GLORIOUS WEEKEND WITH CHILDLIKE WONDER STEMMING FROM THE JUBILATION OF EASTER.

HAPPY HUNTING

On this festive day, host a merry alfresco affair planned with the whole family in mind. This most-anticipated holiday epitomizes spring's sense of renewal, and an organic mix of décor brings it to life with the help of pastel flora and verdant accompaniments. Stock, fern, and hydrangeas soften the hearth of a rustic stone fireplace while roses, ranunculus, and Queen Anne's lace keep company along the mantel with ornamental egg-filled nests. Linens introduce dynamic patterns; china bearing bamboo borders and resembling artful cabbage leaves helps further the natural motif inspired by the open-air setting. As children with baskets in hand take to the yard in search of treats and treasures, guests can indulge in simple bites like creamy Granola Parfait Cups and flavorful mini quiches. A delectable duo makes for a crowd-pleasing finale: macaroons dotted with colorful sprinkles and a pretty-in-pink Raspberry Cloud Cake.

Perfect Parties | 183

DARLING DETAILS

An abundance of themed accents evokes the reason for the revelry, with bunnies, eggs, and more incorporated throughout. A stone planter in the shape of a rabbit graces the table's center with a copious blend of garden and sweetheart roses, peonies, and beyond. Smaller arrangements in bud vases mingle with potted plants and stylized groupings of carrots and radishes. Presented in dainty cups atop beds of moss, decorative eggs offer a creative canvas to display the menu. At day's end, little ones hold tight to their baskets brimming with bounty, making memories that will stay with them long after.

Perfect Parties

Granola Parfait Cups
MAKES 12

2 cups old-fashioned oats
½ cup finely chopped pecans
¼ cup sweetened flaked coconut
1 teaspoon ground cinnamon
½ teaspoon kosher salt
½ teaspoon ground ginger
1 large egg
¼ cup creamy peanut butter
4 tablespoons honey, divided
2 (7-ounce) containers plain Greek yogurt
1 (8-ounce) container mascarpone cheese
3 large fresh strawberries, quartered

1. Preheat oven to 350°. Spray a 12-cup muffin pan with baking spray with flour.
2. In a large bowl, stir together oats, pecans, coconut, cinnamon, salt, and ginger. Stir in egg, peanut butter, and 2 tablespoons honey until well combined. Divide granola mixture among prepared muffin cups, about ¼ cup each, pressing into bottom and about three-fourths up sides.
3. Bake until golden, about 13 minutes. Let cool completely in pan on a wire rack. Remove from pan.
4. In a medium bowl, stir together yogurt, mascarpone, and remaining 2 tablespoons honey. Divide yogurt mixture among granola cups. Top with strawberries, and serve.

Mini Zucchini-Herb Quiches
MAKES 12

1 (14.1-ounce) box refrigerated piecrusts
4 large eggs
½ cup heavy whipping cream
1 tablespoon chopped fresh basil
1 tablespoon chopped fresh oregano
2 teaspoons chopped fresh chives
½ teaspoon kosher salt
¼ teaspoon garlic powder
¼ teaspoon ground black pepper
½ cup shredded sharp white Cheddar cheese, divided
½ cup zucchini thinly sliced into half-moons
Garnish: chopped fresh basil, fresh oregano, fresh chives, flaked sea salt, ground black pepper

1. Position oven rack in bottom third of oven. Preheat oven to 425°.
2. On a lightly floured surface, unroll piecrusts. Using a 4-inch round cutter, cut 12 circles, rerolling scraps as needed. Place into cups of a 12-cup muffin pan, pressing into bottom and up sides.
3. In a medium bowl, whisk together eggs, cream, basil, oregano, chives, kosher salt, garlic powder, and pepper. Stir in ¼ cup cheese. Divide among muffin cups. Top with zucchini slices, and sprinkle with remaining ¼ cup cheese.
4. Bake until golden brown and a wooden pick inserted in center comes out clean, about 13 minutes. Let cool for at least 10 minutes before serving. Garnish with basil, oregano, chives, sea salt, and pepper, if desired.

Easter Macaroons

MAKES ABOUT 18 COOKIES

1 (14-ounce) package sweetened flaked coconut
½ cup sugar
2 tablespoons all-purpose flour
1 tablespoon lemon zest
½ teaspoon kosher salt
4 large egg whites, room temperature
¼ teaspoon almond extract
Pastel sprinkles, for topping

1. Preheat oven to 350°. Line a baking sheet with parchment paper.
2. In a large bowl, stir together coconut, sugar, flour, zest, and salt. Add egg whites and extract, stirring until well combined.
3. Scoop 2 tablespoons cookie batter, and place at least 1 inch apart on prepared baking pan. Sprinkle tops with sprinkles.
4. Bake until bottoms are golden, about 18 minutes. Let cool completely on pan.

Raspberry Cloud Cake

MAKES 1 (9-INCH) CAKE

2 cups unsalted butter, softened
4 cups sugar
8 large eggs, room temperature
2½ cups fresh raspberries
1 tablespoon vanilla extract
6 cups cake flour
2 tablespoons baking powder
2 teaspoons kosher salt
2 cups whole buttermilk, room temperature
2 to 3 drops red food coloring
Raspberry Frosting (recipe follows)
Garnish: fresh raspberries, edible organic flowers

1. Preheat oven to 350°. Spray 3 (9-inch) round tall-sided cake pans with baking spray with flour. Line bottoms with parchment paper.
2. In the bowl of a stand mixer fitted with the paddle attachment, beat butter and sugar at medium speed until fluffy, 3 to 4 minutes, stopping to scrape sides of bowl. Add eggs, one at a time, beating well after each addition. Beat in raspberries and vanilla.
3. In a medium bowl, whisk together flour, baking powder, and salt. In a small bowl, combine buttermilk and food coloring. Gradually add flour mixture to butter mixture alternately with buttermilk, beginning and ending with flour mixture, beating until combined after each addition. Divide batter among prepared pans, smoothing tops with an offset spatula.
4. Bake until a wooden pick inserted in center comes out clean, 35 to 40 minutes. Let cool in pans on a wire rack for 10 minutes. Remove from pans, and let cool completely on wire racks.
5. Spread Raspberry Frosting between layers and on top and sides of cake. Garnish with raspberries and edible flowers, if desired.

RASPBERRY FROSTING

MAKES ABOUT 7½ CUPS

¼ cup whole buttermilk
½ cup fresh raspberries, strained
2½ cups unsalted butter, softened
⅛ teaspoon kosher salt
7 cups confectioners' sugar
1 drop red food coloring (optional)

1. In a medium glass measuring cup, stir together buttermilk and juice from strained raspberries.
2. In the bowl of a stand mixer fitted with the paddle attachment, beat butter and salt at low speed until smooth, 1 to 2 minutes. Slowly add one-fourth of confectioners' sugar and one-fourth of buttermilk mixture, beating until smooth; continue alternately adding confectioners' sugar and buttermilk mixture until frosting is smooth and fluffy. Scrape sides of bowl, and increase mixer speed to medium, beating for 5 minutes. Add food coloring (if using).

Basket of Goodies

Perfect for springtime tables—especially Easter settings—this simple napkin fold will brighten the spirits of gathered family and friends. Follow these five steps to recreate a tabletop accent that appeals to both little ones and those young at heart.

1. Fold any square linen napkin of your choice diagonally into a triangle.

2. Fold the bottom edge up about halfway to the top point.

3. Fold one corner across the center, and repeat with the opposite corner, letting the excess wrap all the way around.

4. Carefully roll the pointed portion down to create an open basket, tucking any loose fabric beneath the rim.

5. Nestle a clear glass container into the napkin's center and then fill with small candies for a delightful favor guests can enjoy.

Perfect Parties | 191

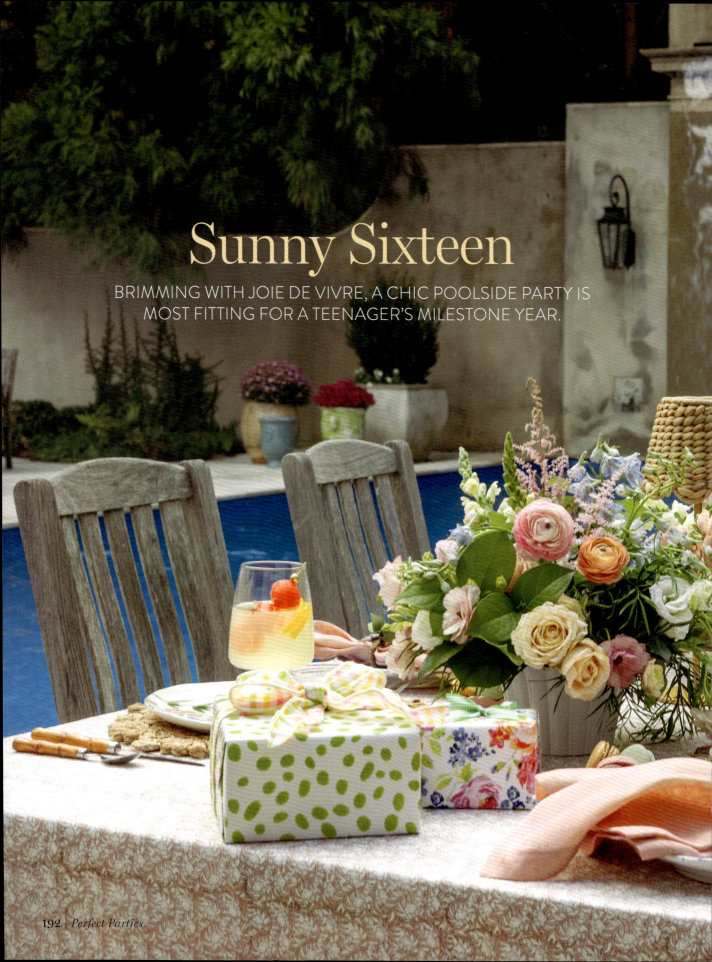

Sunny Sixteen

BRIMMING WITH JOIE DE VIVRE, A CHIC POOLSIDE PARTY IS MOST FITTING FOR A TEENAGER'S MILESTONE YEAR.

Perfect Parties | 193

FLOUNCING FUN

Make a splash for the special teen's day with a table bursting with color. Hand-painted blooms enhance dinner plates framed by a woven flower-edged place mat. Blush napkins and a block-print tablecloth brighten the setting, as three sprightly arrangements of pink and orange ranunculus, garden roses, lisianthus, delphinium, and lush greenery echo the scheme. While lounging after a swim, nosh on spiced snack mix, Bacon Cheeseburger Sliders, and fruit skewers; jazz up lemonade with specialty syrups and fresh add-ins. When presents are passed and the candles are added to a showstopping chocolate-and-raspberry cake, the birthday girl makes a wish, envisioning the exciting year ahead.

Barbecue Snack Mix
MAKES ABOUT 18 CUPS

¼ cup butter, melted
3 tablespoons barbecue sauce
2 tablespoons Worcestershire sauce
2 tablespoons light corn syrup
1 (1-ounce) envelope ranch dressing mix
1 tablespoon smoked paprika
¼ teaspoon powdered mustard
⅛ teaspoon ground red pepper
4 cups corn-and-rice cereal*
4 cups corn cereal squares*
3 cups bite-size Cheddar cheese crackers*
3 cups baked snack crackers*
3 cups small pretzel twists
1 cup roasted peanuts

1. Preheat oven to 250°. In a small bowl, whisk together butter, barbecue sauce, Worcestershire, corn syrup, ranch mix, paprika, mustard, and red pepper.
2. In a large roasting pan, combine cereals, crackers, pretzels, and peanuts. Stir butter mixture into cereal mixture until well coated.
3. Bake for 60 to 75 minutes, stirring every 15 minutes, until crispy. Spread in a single layer on wax paper to cool. Store in an airtight container for up to 1 week.

We used Crispix and Corn Chex cereals, Cheez-Its, and Wheat Thins Original Crackers.

Bacon Cheeseburger Sliders
MAKES 14

2 pounds ground chuck
1 pound bacon, cooked, crumbled, and drained
2 tablespoons Worcestershire sauce
½ teaspoon kosher salt
½ teaspoon ground black pepper
14 slices Colby-Jack cheese
14 slider buns

1. Spray grill rack with nonstick nonflammable cooking spray. Preheat grill to medium-high heat (350° to 400°).
2. In a large bowl, stir together ground chuck, bacon, Worcestershire, salt, and pepper. Shape mixture into 14 patties.
3. Grill for 5 to 7 minutes per side or until a thermometer inserted in center registers 160°. Top patties with cheese slices, remove from grill, and let stand for 10 minutes. Serve on buns with desired toppings.

Fruit Skewers with Cheesecake Dip
SERVES 8 TO 10

½ small cantaloupe, peeled, seeded, and cut into 1-inch pieces
½ small honeydew, peeled, seeded, and cut into 1-inch pieces
½ small pineapple, peeled, cored, and cut into 1-inch pieces
1 quart fresh strawberries, halved
24 (6-inch) wooden skewers

Perfect Parties | 197

- 1 (8-ounce) package ⅓-less-fat cream cheese
- ¼ cup milk
- ¼ cup confectioners' sugar
- ½ teaspoon vanilla extract

1. Thread 1 piece each of cantaloupe, honeydew, pineapple, and strawberry onto skewers.
2. In the bowl of a stand mixer fitted with the paddle attachment, beat cream cheese and milk at medium speed until smooth. Beat in confectioners' sugar and vanilla until smooth. Serve dip with fruit.

Chocolate Cake with Fluffy Raspberry Frosting
MAKES 1 (9-INCH) CAKE

- 1 cup butter, softened
- ¾ cup firmly packed brown sugar
- ½ cup granulated sugar
- 3 large eggs
- 2½ cups cake flour*
- ¾ cup unsweetened cocoa powder
- 1½ teaspoons baking soda
- ½ teaspoon kosher salt
- 1½ cups buttermilk
- ½ cup sour cream
- Fluffy Raspberry Frosting (recipe follows)
- Garnish: fresh raspberries

1. Preheat oven to 350°. Spray 3 (9-inch) cake pans with nonstick baking spray with flour.
2. In the bowl of a stand mixer fitted with the paddle attachment, beat butter and sugars at medium speed until fluffy. Add eggs, one at a time, beating well after each addition.
3. In a medium bowl, combine flour, cocoa powder, baking soda, and salt. Gradually add flour mixture to butter mixture, alternately with buttermilk, beginning and ending with flour mixture, beating just until combined after each addition. Stir in sour cream. Pour batter into prepared pans, and bake for 13 to 17 minutes or until a wooden pick inserted in center comes out clean. Cool in pans for 10 minutes. Remove from pans, and cool completely on wire racks.
4. Spread Fluffy Raspberry Frosting in between layers and on top and sides of cake. Garnish with fresh raspberries, if desired.

*We used Swans Down Cake Flour.

FLUFFY RASPBERRY FROSTING
MAKES ABOUT 6 CUPS

- 1 (6-ounce) package fresh raspberries
- 1 tablespoon granulated sugar
- 1 teaspoon fresh lemon juice
- 1 cup butter, softened
- 1 (8-ounce) package cream cheese, softened
- 7 cups confectioners' sugar

1. In a small saucepan, combine raspberries, granulated sugar, and lemon juice. Bring to a boil over medium-high heat; reduce heat, and simmer 3 minutes, stirring frequently. Press mixture through a fine-mesh sieve, discarding solids. Cool to room temperature.
2. In the bowl of a stand mixer fitted with the paddle attachment, beat butter, cream cheese, and raspberry syrup at medium speed until combined. Gradually add confectioners' sugar, beating until smooth.

Itty Bitty Pretty One

WELCOME A FAMILY'S NEW ADDITION WITH A SETTING INSPIRED BY HANS CHRISTIAN ANDERSON'S BELOVED TALE OF *THUMBELINA*, THE PINT-SIZE ANSWER TO A BIG-TIME WISH.

HEART'S DESIRE

Imagine the happiness when Thumbelina's mother discovered her tiny wish-come-true curled in the petals of a beautiful flower! For this baby banquet, replicate the fictional child's botanical beginnings with napkins folded in the shape of buds. Thumbprint cookies are an ideal choice for refreshments, as are two types of savory tea sandwiches made from garden-fresh ingredients and garnished to perfection. Complete the menu of mini morsels with crisp veggies and a creamy dip.

Perfect Parties | 203

Green Goddess Dressing
MAKES 2 CUPS

1 cup plain Greek yogurt
¾ cup mayonnaise
½ cup chopped fresh parsley
¼ cup chopped fresh tarragon
¼ cup chopped fresh chives
2 tablespoons lemon juice
2 anchovy fillets, chopped
1 clove garlic, chopped
½ teaspoon kosher salt
¼ teaspoon ground black pepper
Garnish: extra-virgin olive oil, pepper
Fresh vegetables, to serve

1. Place yogurt, mayonnaise, parsley, tarragon, chives, lemon juice, anchovies, garlic, salt, and pepper in the pitcher of a blender. Blend until smooth. Refrigerate until ready to serve.
2. Spoon dip into a serving bowl. Garnish with olive oil and pepper, if desired. Serve with fresh vegetables.

Spring Garden Tea Sandwiches
MAKES 12

½ cup unsalted butter, softened
1 tablespoon chopped fresh chives
¼ teaspoon kosher salt
⅛ teaspoon ground black pepper
12 slices pumpernickel tea bread
6 radishes, thinly sliced
½ cup alfalfa sprouts

1. In a small bowl, stir butter until smooth. Add chives, salt, and pepper, stirring to combine.
2. Spread a layer of butter mixture onto each bread slice. Top with sliced radishes and sprouts. Serve immediately.

Herbed Chicken Salad Tea Sandwiches
MAKES 15

¼ cup plus 1 tablespoon mayonnaise
¼ cup plus 1 tablespoon sour cream
2 tablespoons chopped fresh parsley

2 tablespoons chopped green onion
1 tablespoon chopped fresh tarragon
1 tablespoon chopped fresh dill
2 teaspoons lemon juice
½ teaspoon kosher salt
¼ teaspoon ground black pepper
Pinch garlic powder
2 cups finely chopped cooked chicken
¼ cup golden raisins
¼ cup toasted sliced almonds
10 slices white sandwich bread
½ cup thinly sliced cucumber
Garnish: thinly sliced cucumber, chive

1. In a large bowl, stir together mayonnaise, sour cream, parsley, green onion, tarragon, dill, lemon juice, salt, pepper, and garlic powder. Add chicken, raisins, and almonds, stirring to combine.
2. Spread a thick, even layer of chicken salad onto 5 bread slices. Evenly divide cucumber slices among bread slices. Top each with remaining bread slice. Using a bread knife, cut crust from bread; discard. Cut each sandwich into 3 rectangular shapes.
3. Garnish each tea sandwich with thinly sliced cucumbers, or wrap each with a chive, if desired.

Almond Thumbprint Cookies

MAKES 36

1 cup unsalted butter, softened
½ cup firmly packed light brown sugar
2 cups all-purpose flour
1 cup almonds, toasted and finely ground
1 teaspoon kosher salt
2 teaspoons vanilla extract
¼ cup strawberry jam, warmed
¼ cup apricot jam, warmed

1. Preheat oven to 350°. Line two baking sheets with parchment paper, and set aside.
2. In a stand mixer fitted with the paddle attachment, beat butter and sugar until light and fluffy, about 4 minutes. Gradually add flour, ground almonds, salt, and vanilla; mix until fully incorporated.
3. Using a tablespoon scoop, roll dough into 1-inch balls. Using your thumb or the handle of a wooden spoon, make an indentation in the center of each ball. Bake for 10 minutes.
4. Remove from oven, and place ½ teaspoon warmed strawberry or apricot jam in center of each cookie. Bake until cookies are fully cooked and lightly golden brown around the edges, 5 minutes more. Let cool completely.

Perfect Parties

Shapely Finesse

Follow our step-by-step instructions to fold linen napkins into tabletop accents that call to mind lovely water lilies. This finishing touch is perfect for a ladies' luncheon, bridal brunch, or baby shower.

1. Lay flat a square napkin and fold each corner to meet at the center, pressing folds as you work to create a square.

2. Flip the napkin over and fold each corner to the center again, pressing each fold as you work.

3. Press down on the center of the napkin to hold the corners in place. Reach underneath and pull up each corner to create the water lily petals. Push the center of each petal back gently to help its shape.

Perfect Parties | 207

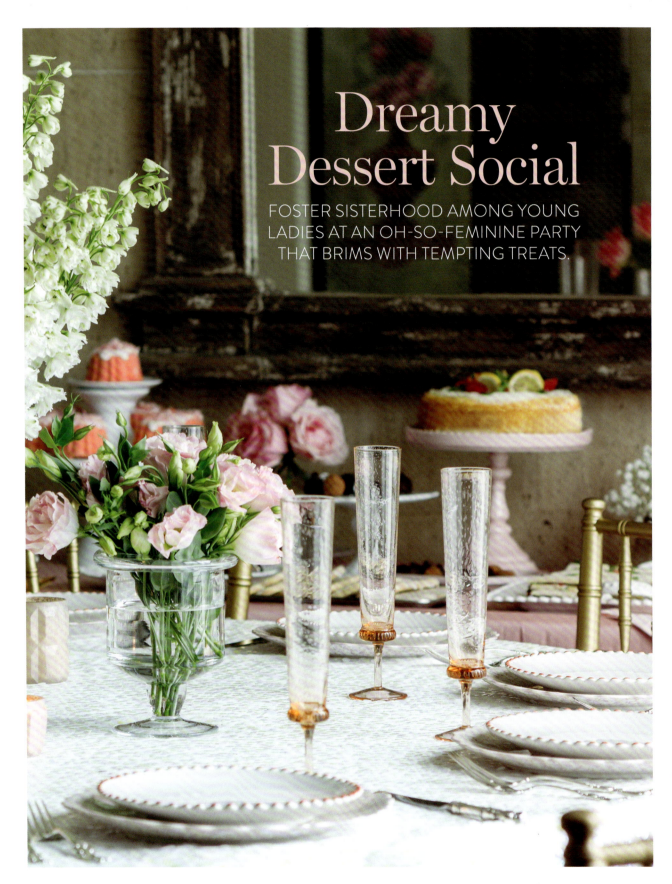

Dreamy Dessert Social

FOSTER SISTERHOOD AMONG YOUNG LADIES AT AN OH-SO-FEMININE PARTY THAT BRIMS WITH TEMPTING TREATS.

BLUSHING BEAUTY

For Valentine's Day—or any reason at all—make girlfriends feel like the belles of the ball for the afternoon. Shades of pink and cream set the tone for this frilly affair, where an apropos table skirt of floor-length tulle extends a grand welcome. A mix of vases holding single flower varieties not only creates an easy centerpiece but also can be readily dispersed at party's end to send home with pals so dear. While certainly not required, dancing shoes and twirly dresses will only add to the glitz and glamour. Delicious tea sandwiches feature fresh strawberries and basil, while a classic Cobb salad balances the lineup of cookies, cakes, and chocolate truffles to come.

Refreshing Cobb Salad
MAKES 8 SERVINGS

1 head romaine lettuce, shredded
8 hard-cooked eggs, quartered
8 slices thick-cut bacon, cooked and chopped
3 large tomatoes, chopped
3 avocados, chopped
1 English cucumber, chopped
6 cups deli-roasted chicken
1 (8-ounce) container feta cheese, crumbled
½ cup fresh parsley leaves
Orange Poppy Seed Dressing (recipe follows)

1. Place lettuce on 2 large platters. Arrange eggs, bacon, tomatoes, avocado, cucumber, chicken, and cheese in rows on top of lettuce. Sprinkle with parsley. Serve with Orange Poppy Seed Dressing.

ORANGE POPPY SEED DRESSING
MAKES ABOUT 1⅓ CUPS

½ cup olive oil
⅓ cup fresh orange juice
3 tablespoons fresh lemon juice
3 tablespoons white wine vinegar
2 tablespoons honey
3 teaspoons poppy seeds
2 teaspoons honey Dijon mustard
1½ teaspoons kosher salt
1 teaspoon orange zest

1. In a small bowl, whisk together all ingredients. Dressing will keep refrigerated for up to 1 week.

Strawberry Tea Sandwiches
MAKES 12

1 (8-ounce) package cream cheese, softened
⅓ cup mayonnaise

¼ teaspoon salt
3 tablespoons finely chopped fresh basil
24 slices thin white bread, crusts removed
15 sliced fresh strawberries
Garnish: fresh baby basil leaves

1. In the work bowl of a food processor, place cream cheese, mayonnaise, and salt. Process until smooth, stopping to scrape sides of bowl. Stir in basil.
2. Spread cream cheese mixture onto half of bread slices. Top with sliced strawberries. Cover with remaining bread slices. Cut into triangles. Cover with a damp paper towel, and store in a sealed container to keep bread from drying out. Garnish with basil, if desired.

Glazed Sweetheart Cookies

MAKES 36

1 cup butter, softened
1 cup granulated sugar
1 teaspoon vanilla extract
1 large egg
2¼ cups all-purpose flour
¼ teaspoon kosher salt
2 cups confectioners' sugar
2 tablespoons meringue powder
¼ cup water
Edible white glitter

1. Preheat oven to 350°. Spray baking sheets with baking spray with flour.
2. In the bowl of a stand mixer fitted with the paddle attachment, beat butter, granulated sugar, and vanilla at medium speed until creamy, 3 to 4 minutes, stopping to scrape sides of bowl. Add egg, beating well. In a medium bowl, whisk together flour and salt. Gradually add flour mixture to butter mixture, beating just until combined.
3. Divide dough into 2 equal portions. Shape each portion into a disk. Wrap in plastic wrap, and refrigerate for 10 minutes.
4. On a heavily floured surface, roll one dough disk to ⅛-inch thickness. Using a 3-inch heart-shaped cutter, cut dough, rerolling scraps as necessary. Place 2 inches apart on prepared pans. Repeat with remaining dough.
5. Bake until edges are lightly browned, 10 to 12 minutes. Let cool on pans for 5 minutes. Remove from pans, and let cool completely on wire racks.
6. In a medium bowl, whisk together confectioners' sugar, meringue powder, and ¼ cup water. Brush cookies with mixture, and sprinkle with edible glitter.

Creamy Lemon Cheesecake

MAKES 1 (9-INCH) CAKE

2 cups crushed shortbread cookies
¼ cup unsalted butter, melted
5 (8-ounce) packages cream cheese, softened
2 cups sugar
2 tablespoons all-purpose flour
1½ teaspoons vanilla extract
4 large eggs
⅓ cup heavy whipping cream
1 tablespoon lemon zest
1 (16-ounce) container sour cream, room temperature
Garnish: lemon slices, fresh mint leaves, fresh strawberries

1. Preheat oven to 350°. Spray a 9-inch springform pan with baking spray with flour.
2. In a medium bowl, stir together crushed cookies and melted butter. Press mixture into bottom of prepared pan.
3. Bake until golden brown, 8 to 10 minutes. Let cool on a wire rack for 30 minutes. Reduce temperature to 325°.
4. In the bowl of a stand mixer, beat cream cheese at medium speed until creamy. Gradually add sugar, flour, and vanilla, beating until smooth. Add eggs, one at a time, beating just until combined after each addition. Beat in cream and zest. Pour into prepared crust.
5. Bake until soft set, about 1 hour and 10 minutes.
6. In a medium bowl, combine sour cream and remaining ⅓ cup sugar. Gently spread over cheesecake. Bake for 5 minutes. Turn oven off, and leave cheesecake in oven with door closed for 20 minutes. Remove from oven, and place on a wire rack. Gently run a sharp knife around edges of cheesecake to release sides. Let cool at room temperature for 2 hours. Cover and refrigerate overnight. Garnish with lemon slices, mint, and strawberries, if desired.

Almond Custard Tarts

MAKES 12

1¼ cups all-purpose flour
1 cup slivered almonds, toasted
¼ cup sugar
½ teaspoon salt
¾ cup unsalted butter
2 to 3 tablespoons ice water
Almond Custard (recipe follows)
Sweetened whipped cream, fresh raspberries, fresh mint leaves

1. In the work bowl of a food processor, place flour, almonds, sugar, and salt. Pulse until almonds are finely ground. Add butter, and pulse until mixture is crumbly. With processor running, add water in a slow, steady stream until a ball begins to form.
2. Spray 12 (3-inch) brioche molds with baking spray with flour. Divide almond mixture among prepared pans, pressing gently into bottom and up sides. Place pans on a large jelly roll pan. Refrigerate for 20 minutes.
3. Preheat oven to 400°. Bake until golden brown, about 20 minutes. Let cool in pans for 10 minutes. Remove from pans, and let cool completely on wire racks.
4. Just before serving, divide Almond Custard among tart shells. Top with whipped cream, raspberries, and mint.

ALMOND CUSTARD

MAKES 3 CUPS

2 cups half-and-half
¾ cup sugar
⅓ cup all-purpose flour
4 large eggs
2 tablespoons unsalted butter
½ teaspoon almond extract

1. In a medium saucepan, whisk together half-and-half, sugar, flour, and eggs until smooth. Cook over medium heat, stirring

Perfect Parties | 215

constantly, until thickened, about 10 minutes. Remove from heat; stir in butter and almond extract. Transfer to a medium bowl. Place a sheet of plastic wrap directly on surface of custard. Refrigerate for 30 minutes.

Chocolate Truffles
MAKES ABOUT 60

4 (4-ounce) bars dark (60%) chocolate, chopped
1½ cups heavy whipping cream
⅓ cup seedless raspberry preserves
½ teaspoon kosher salt
For rolling: unsweetened cocoa powder, confectioners' sugar, chocolate jimmies, dark chocolate melting wafers*

1. Place chopped chocolate in a medium bowl. In a small saucepan, heat cream, preserves, and salt over medium heat until bubbles begin to form. Pour over chocolate. Cover and let stand for 5 minutes. Stir chocolate mixture until smooth. Cover and refrigerate until firm, about 2 hours.
2. Using a 1-inch scoop, scoop chocolate mixture, and place on parchment paper. Making sure your hands stay cool, roll chocolate into balls. Refrigerate until firm, about 10 minutes. Roll one-fourth of truffles in cocoa, and place on a parchment-lined baking sheet. Refrigerate until set, about 15 minutes. Roll one-fourth of truffles in confectioners' sugar, and one-fourth of truffles in chocolate jimmies.
3. Melt 1 cup chocolate melting wafers according to package directions. Dip remaining one-fourth of truffles, one at a time, in melted chocolate. Remove with a fork, and tap to remove excess chocolate. Using a knife, gently slide truffles onto prepared pan. Let stand until set.

*We used Ghirardelli.

Petite Strawberry Coconut Cakes
MAKES 12

2 cups unsalted butter, softened
2½ cups sugar
1 (3-ounce) box strawberry gelatin
6 large eggs
4 cups all-purpose flour
½ cup whole milk
White Glaze (recipe follows)
Pink Coconut (recipe follows)

1. Preheat oven to 325°. Spray 12 mini Bundt pans with baking spray with flour.
2. In the bowl of a stand mixer, beat butter at medium speed until creamy. Gradually add sugar, beating until fluffy, 3 to 4 minutes, stopping to scrape sides of bowl. Add gelatin; beat for 1 minute. Add eggs, one at a time, beating just until combined after each addition.
3. With mixer on low speed, gradually add flour to butter mixture alternately with milk, beginning and ending with flour, beating just until combined after each addition. Spoon batter into prepared pans, filling ¾ inch full.
4. Bake until a wooden pick inserted near center comes out clean, about 25 minutes. Let cool in pans for 10 minutes. Remove from pans, and let cool completely. Drizzle White Glaze over cooled cakes. Sprinkle with Pink Coconut.

WHITE GLAZE
MAKES 1¼ CUPS

2 cups confectioners' sugar, sifted
3 tablespoons light corn syrup
3 to 4 tablespoons whole milk

1. In a medium bowl, whisk together all ingredients until smooth.

PINK COCONUT
MAKES 1¼ CUPS

1¼ cups sweetened flaked coconut
2 to 3 drops liquid red food coloring

1. In a large resealable bag, place coconut and food coloring. Seal bag, and shake until food coloring coats coconut and is bright pink. Store in an airtight container for up to 1 week.

Perfect Parties | 217

Recipe Index

BEVERAGES
Cherry-Lemon Sparkler **34**
Citrus Mint Sweet Tea **82**
Elderflower Rosé Wine Spritzer **26**
Elderflower Royale **120**
Honeysuckle Sweet Tea **102**
Lavender French 75 **128**
Lavender Pink Lemonade Punch **150**
Lemonade with Mint and Honey **62**
Peach-Infused Sweet Tea **52**
Rose Water Lemonade **43**
Strawberry Cheesecake Smoothies **178**
Strawberry Bellinis **112**
White Russian Coffee **96**

STARTERS AND SNACKS
Bacon and Green Onion Dip **137**
Barbecue Snack Mix **197**
Biscuit Crostini with Smoked Salmon Rosettes **160**
Cheese Wafers **111**
Chicken Salad Lettuce Cups **111**
Elegant Pickled Shrimp **120**
Fig, Ham, and Asparagus Pastry Bundles **84**
Fruit Skewers with Cheesecake Dip **197**
Granola Parfait Cups **186**
Homemade Potato Chips **137**
Mini Crab Quiches **26**
Mini Mushroom Tarts **111**
Mini Zucchini-Herb Quiches **186**
Prosciutto and Fig Flatbread **137**
Rainbow Fruit Cups with Vanilla Honey **176**
Shrimp Toast Points **52**

MAIN DISHES
Baked Pretzel Chicken Tenders **176**
Cilantro-Lime Shrimp Lettuce Wraps **61**
Classic Chicken à la King **54**
Creamed Tarragon Chicken and Bacon Vol-au-Vents **120**
Gingered Chicken Skewers **102**
Heirloom Tomato Shrimp and Grits **128**
Vidalia Onion-Bacon Tart **72**
Wine-Braised Short Ribs **94**

SOUPS AND SANDWICHES
Asparagus-Avocado Bisque **72**
Bacon Cheeseburger Sliders **197**
Chilled Peach Soup **43**
Herbed Chicken Salad Tea Sandwiches **204**
Peanut Butter and Jam Flower Sandwiches **168**
Roasted Red Pepper Soup with Shrimp **34**
Spring Garden Tea Sandwiches **204**
Strawberry Tea Sandwiches **212**
Turkey Sliders with Red Onion Jam **137**

SALADS, SIDES, AND BREAD
Asparagus with Lemon and Parmesan **96**
Baby Carrots with Fresh Herb Dip **160**
Browned Butter–Herb Noodles **96**
Dill–Sour Cream Rolls **43**
Fresh Fruit Salad **128**
Heirloom Tomato Salad **52**
Herb Butter Smashed Peas **74**
Lemon-Garlic Snap Peas **62**
Melon Salad with Vanilla-Honey Dressing **102**
Orange and Radicchio Salad **94**
Refreshing Cobb Salad **212**
Seasoned Biscuits **160**
Shaved Spring Salad **82**
Smoked Salmon Pasta Salad with Peas and Arugula **44**
Spring Garden Seven-Layer Salad **28**
Sweet and Spicy Jalapeño Slaw **61**
Watercress Salad with Lemon and Almonds **34**

CONDIMENTS AND SALAD DRESSINGS
Buttermilk Ranch Dip **176**
Green Goddess Dressing **204**
Honey Mustard–Poppy Seed Dressing **82**
Orange Poppy Seed Dressing **212**
Red Onion Jam **138**
Sweet Chili Sauce **52**

DESSERTS
Almond Custard Tarts **215**
Almond Roca **150**
Almond Thumbprint Cookies **205**
Angel Food Cupcakes with Swiss Meringue Buttercream **37**
Apricot Crumble Bars **28**
Birthday Flower Cupcakes **178**
Chocolate Cake with Fluffy Raspberry Frosting **198**
Chocolate Truffles **216**
Chocolate-Brandy Truffles **148**
Coconut-Mango Semifreddo **62**
Creamy Lemon Cheesecake **215**
Easter Macaroons **188**
Glazed Sweetheart Cookies **213**
Golden Anniversary Cake **122**
Lemon Chiffon Cake **54**
Lemon Honey Cheesecake Bars **104**
Lemon Sugar Cookies **148**
Lemon-Blackberry Petits Fours **161**
Lemon-Lavender Sablés **74**
Mini Almond Bundt Cakes with Lavender Glaze **84**
Petite Strawberry Coconut Cakes **216**
Pink Cotton Candy Macarons **169**
Pink Grapefruit Jellies **150**
Pink Heart Scones **168**
Raspberry Cloud Cake **188**
Raspberry Panna Cotta **44**
Rhubarb Pavlovas **111**
Strawberry Pie Love Letters **97**
Strawberry Swirl Fudge **138**
Vanilla Mini Cupcakes with Vanilla Buttercream **168**
White Chocolate-Covered Strawberries **162**

FROSTINGS, GLAZES, AND SWEET ADDITIONS
Almond Custard **215**
Classic Simple Syrup **130**
Fluffy Raspberry Frosting **198**
Lavender Simple Syrup **130, 150**
Lemon Buttercream **162**
Lemon Glaze **54**
Meringue Powder Icing **148**
Pink Coconut **216**
Raspberry Frosting **188**
Raspberry Simple Syrup **130**
Rhubarb Compote **112**
Swiss Meringue Buttercream **37**
Sweet Whipped Cream **97**
Vanilla Buttercream **169**
Vanilla Buttercream Frosting **122**
White Chocolate Ganache **169**
White Glaze **216**

Credits & Acknowledgments

EDITORIAL

EDITORIAL DIRECTOR, LIFESTYLE Lisa Frederick

MANAGING EDITOR Ashley Shaw
SENIOR FEATURES EDITOR Kate Lorio
FEATURES EDITOR Claire Pool
SENIOR COPY EDITOR, LIFESTYLE Rhonda Lee Lother
EDITORIAL ASSISTANT Kara Mautz
EDITORIAL CONTRIBUTORS Marie Baxley, Karen Callaway, Elizabeth Bonner Czapski, Kathleen Whaley

SENIOR PHOTOGRAPHER John O'Hagan
PHOTOGRAPHERS Jim Bathie, Kyle Carpenter, Stephanie Welbourne Steele
CONTRIBUTING PHOTOGRAPHERS Stephen DeVries, William Dickey, Mac Jamieson, Steve Rizzo, Marcy Black Simpson

SENIOR DIGITAL IMAGING SPECIALIST Delisa McDaniel

CREATIVE DIRECTOR, LIFESTYLE Melissa Sturdivant Smith
ADMINISTRATIVE SR. ART DIRECTOR Tracy Wood-Franklin
ART DIRECTOR Karissa Brown

SENIOR STYLIST Sidney Bragiel
STYLISTS Maghan Armstrong, Courtni Bodiford, Maggie Hill, Donna Nichols
CONTRIBUTING STYLISTS Mary Beth Jones, Tracey MacMillan Russell, Lily Simpson, Dorothy Walton

TEST KITCHEN DIRECTOR Laura Crandall
FOOD STYLISTS/RECIPE DEVELOPERS Ola Agbodza, Aaron Conrad, Katie Moon Dickerson, Kathleen Kanen, Vanessa Rocchio, Amanda Stabile, Izzie Turner
CONTRIBUTING RECIPE DEVELOPERS/FOOD STYLISTS Becca Cummins, Melissa Gray, Ashley Jones, Kellie Gerber Kelley, Janet Lambert, Erin Merhar, Elizabeth Stringer, Anna Theoktisto, Loren Wood
TEST KITCHEN ASSISTANT/PREP COOK Madison Harvel

Over the years, we have been blessed by the generosity and hospitality of many homeowners, as well as by our friends at some of the finest stores and companies in the world. To them, we offer our sincerest gratitude for their help with the contents of this special volume.

Abigails	Busatti	Joanna Buchanan
Amanda Lindroth	Caskata	Julia Amory
Annieglass	CB Lifestyle	Juliska
Anthropologie	Crown Linen Designs	Katherine Young Home
April Cornell	Deborah Rhodes	Kim Seybert
Arte Italica	Dogwood Hill	Mrs. Alice
At Home Furnishings	The Enchanted Home	Replacements, Ltd.
Beatriz Ball	Estelle Colored Glass	SFERRA
Blue Pheasant	Fenwick Fields	Table Matters
Bodrum	Heather Taylor Home	Two's Company
Bromberg's	Herend	Vietri

> "IT'S NOT THE GRANDEUR OF THE MOMENT; IT IS THE GATHERING.... ENJOY THESE TIMES WITH FRIENDS AND FAMILY—THEY ARE THE MOMENTS WE WILL REMEMBER AND RELIVE IN OUR MINDS."
> —PHYLLIS HOFFMAN DEPIANO, FOUNDER OF HOFFMAN MEDIA
> (1953–2023)